NO NONSENSE GARDENING GUIDE

THE SUCCESSFUL VEGETABLE GARDEN

By the Editors of Garden Way Publishing

Longmeadow Press

THE SUCCESSFUL VEGETABLE GARDEN

Copyright © 1990 by Storey Communications, Inc.

Published by Longmeadow Press, 201 High Ridge Road, Stamford, Connecticut 06904. No part of this book may be reproduced or used in any form or by any means, electronic or mechanical, including photocopying, recording, or by an information storage and retrieval system, without permission in writing from the publisher.

No Nonsense Gardening Guide is a trademark controlled by Longmeadow Press.

ISBN: 0-681-40967-3

Printed in the United States of America

9 8 7 6 5 4 3 2 1

Prepared for Longmeadow Press by Storey Communications, Inc.

President: M. John Storey
Executive VP, Administration: Martha M. Storey
Publisher: Thomas Woll
Series Editor: Benjamin Watson

Cover and inside design by Leslie Morris Noyes
Edited by Seth Rogovoy
Production by Carol Jessop, Joan Genova, Judy Eliason, and Nancy Lamb
Illustrations by Elayne Sears. Illustration on page 42 by David Sylvester.

The name Garden Way Publishing is licensed to Storey Communications, Inc., by Garden Way, Inc.

Cover photograph © Jerry Howard/Positive Images

Contents

THE NO NONSENSE LIBRARY

NO NONSENSE GARDENING GUIDES

Flowering Houseplants
The Successful Vegetable Garden
Using Annuals & Perennials
Landscaping for Beauty
Herbs the Year Round
The Weekend Gardener

OTHER NO NONSENSE GUIDES

Car Guides
Career Guides
Cooking Guides
Financial Guides
Health Guides
Legal Guides
Parenting Guides
Photography Guides
Real Estate Guides
Study Guides
Success Guides
Wine Guides

Chapter 1

Planning the Garden

Seed companies are well aware of the itchiness that gardeners develop as snowdrifts deepen, and they time delivery of their catalogs to coincide with the onset of cabin fever. A common reaction to the glossy pictures and glowing praises of each new variety is to overreact and order more seeds than the entire neighborhood could use. To avoid this, plan your garden carefully.

First of all, decide on the size garden you want.

Next, determine what vegetables your family enjoys. If just one person enjoys beets, does it really make sense to plant an entire row of them?

Also consider the local climate. Eggplant may be a great delicacy, but are chances for success with this vegetable good in an area with a short growing season?

The Garden Planning Chart on page 6 indicates how much seed or how many plants of most popular vegetables are needed to plant a 50-foot row and to produce a season's supply of each vegetable for one person. Distances between rows are also suggested.

Draw up a plan for your garden on a piece of graph paper. Locate the tallest plants near the northern edge of the garden so that they will not shade shorter neighbors.

The row spacing listed in the Garden Planning Chart is the minimum distance required. If your garden soil is rich, the plants will probably be crowded, and you should increase the distance between rows by about 30 percent.

When making out your garden plan, also consider what type of cultivating equipment you will use. If you plan to use a hoe, rows may be spaced irregularly. If you intend to use a rototiller, plan your rows so that the machine will fit between them and won't disturb plants once they have begun growing.

Crop Rotation

You can improve your garden soil and lessen your problems with disease and insects by rotating your garden crops each year.

Think of this when you lay out this year's garden, and refer

GARDEN PLANNING CHART

VEGETABLE	SEEDS OR PLANTS FOR A 50' ROW	DISTANCE BETWEEN ROWS IN INCHES	FEET OF ROW PER PERSON	SPACING BETWEEN PLANTS IN INCHES
Beans, dry	4 oz.	18"	20-30'	6-8"
Beans, shell	4 oz.	18"	30'	8-10"
Beans, snap	4 oz.	18"	30'	2-4"
Beets	½ oz.	12"	10-15'	2-4"
Broccoli	25 plants	24"	5 plants	12-24"
Brussel sprouts	25 plants	24"	5 plants	12-24"
Cabbage	25 plants	24"	10 plants	12-18"
Cauliflower	25 plants	24"	5 plants	14-24"
Carrots	⅛ oz.	12"	10'	1-3"
Corn	1 oz.	24"	25'	9-15"
Cucumbers	¼ oz.	48"	10-15'	12"
Eggplant	25 plants	24"	5 plants	18-36"
Endive	⅛ oz.	18"	10'	8-12"
Kale	⅛ oz.	18"	12'	18-24"
Kohlrabi	⅛ oz.	18"	10'	3-6"
Lettuce, head	⅛ oz.	15"	5-10'	10-15"
Lettuce, leaf	⅛ oz.	12"	5-10'	10-12"
Muskmelons	12 plants	48"	3 plants	12"
Onion sets	1 lb.	12"	10-20'	2-4"
Parsnips	¼ oz.	18"	5-10'	3-6"
Peas	8 oz.	24"	50-100'	1-3"
Peppers	33 plants	18"	5 plants	12-24"
Potatoes	33 plants	30"	50'	9-12"
Pumpkins	¼ oz.	60"	1 hill	36-60"
Radishes	½ oz.	12"	5'	1-2"
Salsify	½ oz.	18"	5'	2-4"
Spinach	½ oz.	15"	20'	2-6"
Squash, summer	¼ oz.	60"	1 hill	24-48"
Squash, winter	½ oz.	60"	3-5 hills	24-40"
Swiss chard	¼ oz.	18"	5'	3-6"
Tomatoes	12-15 plants	30"	5 plants	12-24"
Turnips	¼ oz.	15"	10'	2-6"
Watermelon	30 plants	72"	2-3 hills	72-96"
Zucchini	¼ oz.	60"	1 hill	24-48"

to your plan for rotating crops in following years. That's what makes a record of your garden layout so valuable; you don't have to depend on your memory as you decide where to put those tomato plants next year.

Rotating crops has been practiced on farmland for centuries. It's impossible, however, to design a rotation plan for a vegetable garden that will work as smoothly as one designed for a multiacre farm. The difference is the number of vegetables grown in a relatively small area.

By following a few simple ground rules, though, you can gain some of the advantages of crop rotation, even in the smallest of gardens.

Here are some things to consider:

■ Don't plant the same vegetable in the same location, year after year. And don't follow any member of the cabbage family — cabbage, brussels sprouts, broccoli, cauliflower, collards, kohlrabi, and others — with other plants of the same family. That's how insect and soil problems get started.

■ Take advantage of nitrogen-fixing vegetables like peas and beans, and plant one of the heavy eaters, such as corn, in their place after them.

■ Squeeze in a green manure crop — beans, peas, soybeans, buckwheat, ryegrass, annual rye, or any of the others — when you have space in the garden. Try especially to plant one of these near the end of the growing season.

■ Try to set up a three-year rotation cycle in your garden, to ensure the best results.

COMPANION PLANTING

Companion planting — the growing together of "good" neighbors which benefit one another and the separation of "bad" neighbors — is one of the secrets of a more vigorous (and probably happier) garden. All plants give off root diffusates, which affect other plants either favorably or unfavorably. The onion family, for example, retards the growth of peas and beans but has a beneficial effect on broccoli. Try a "zigzag" planting arrangement to get "friends" closer together. See the following Companion Planting Chart for a roundup of common garden friends and enemies; refer to this list as you plan your garden.

COMPANION PLANTING CHART

FRUIT/ VEGETABLE	FRIENDS	ENEMIES
Beans	Potatoes, beets, (bush beans only), carrots, peas, cauliflower; cabbage (bush), eggplant, cucumbers, corn, radishes (pole), summer savory, celery (bush), strawberries, rosemary, petunia, parsnips (bush), sunflower (bush)	Beets and cabbage family (pole beans only), onion family (both), kohlrabi, sunflowers (pole), gladiolus, fennel
Beets	Bush beans, cabbage, lettuce, onions, kohlrabi, lima beans	Pole beans
Broccoli	Onion family, herbs. See "Cabbage."	See "Cabbage."
Brussels Sprouts	Carrots, herbs	See "Cabbage."
Cabbage Family (including Broccoli, Brussels Sprouts, Cauliflower, etc.)	Beets, carrots, beans (bush), lettuce, spinach, onions, cucumbers, kale, potatoes, celery, herbs (aromatic), dill, sage (repels cabbage butterflies), rosemary, mint, chamomile, nasturtiums	Strawberries, tomatoes, pole beans
Carrots	Beans, peas, tomatoes, onions, leeks, brussels sprouts, peppers, cabbage, leaf lettuce, red radishes, chives, rosemary, sage	Dill, celery, parsnips
Cauliflower	See "Cabbage."	See "Cabbage"
Celery	Cabbage, cauliflower, leeks, tomatoes, bush beans, peas	Carrots, parsnips
Corn	Beans, peas, early potatoes, cucumbers, cantaloupes, squash, cabbage, parsley, pumpkin	None
Cucumbers	Beans, peas, corn, tomatoes, cabbage, lettuce, radishes, sunflowers, dill, nasturtiums	Potatoes, aromatic herbs, sage

FRUIT/ VEGETABLE	FRIENDS	ENEMIES
Eggplant	Beans, peppers	None
Lettuce	Beets, carrots, radishes (leaf), kohlrabi, strawberries, cabbage, onion family (aids lettuce), basil, cucumbers	None
Melons	Corn (cantaloupe)	None
Onion Family	Beets, tomatoes, broccoli, peppers, kohlrabi, lettuce, cabbage, summer savory, carrots, chamomile, parsnips, turnips, leeks, strawberries	Beans, peas, asparagus
Peas	Radishes, carrots, cucumbers, corn, beans, turnips, celery, potatoes	Onion family, gladiolus
Peppers	Tomatoes, eggplant, onions, carrot, parsnips	None
Potatoes	Beans, cabbage, corn, peas, marigolds, eggplant (as a lure for Colorado potato beetle), parsnips	Pumpkin, squash, cucumbers, turnips, rutabagas, tomatoes, sunflowers, raspberry
Pumpkin	Corn, eggplant, radishes	Potatoes
Radishes	Peas, pole beans, leaf lettuce, cucumbers, carrots, lima beans, parsnips, nasturtiums, chervil	None
Spinach	Cabbage, strawberries	None
Squash	Corn, nasturtiums	Potatoes
Tomatoes	Asparagus, peppers, celery, onions, cucumbers, basil, parsley, mint, marigolds, nasturtiums, carrots, chives	Dill, potatoes, cabbage, kohlrabi, fennel
Turnips	Peas and most vegetables, including onion family	Potatoes

9

SUCCESSION PLANTING

There's a tradition among many gardeners that calls for planting the garden on Memorial Day. Everything goes in on that day — onion sets, carrot seeds, tomato and pepper plants, everything.

The result, of course, is the feast-and-famine harvest. All of a sudden, lots of lettuce, then none. The beans all ripen at once, and suddenly you're faced with several unattractive alternatives. You can either gorge yourself and your family, spend long, hot hours preserving, give beans away to the neighbors (who probably have beans of their own), or let the fresh produce go to waste — which is a waste of money and a crying shame.

If you're one of these gardeners, you're missing opportunities to enjoy tender, early lettuce, to give onions a good start before the last frost, and to raise the sweetest peas.

There are many opportunities, too, for fall gardening. Late-planted lettuce, kale, cabbage, brussels sprouts, beets, turnips, broccoli, cauliflower, carrots, Swiss chard, peas, and spinach, will all grow after the first frost, providing delicious garden-to-table meals well into the fall. Even frost-tender vegetables can be started late, giving you last-of-the-season crops of beans, tomatoes, and others.

If you want to be more specific, there's a way to figure out how to get a crop of a certain vegetable before the first frost. It involves simple arithmetic, starting with the first frost date, and working backward. Here's an example, using beans.

First frost date   October 15

    MINUS crops may take longer to mature in fall, 14 days

    MINUS days to maturity (on seed packet), 55 days

    TOTAL days to subtract, 69

Last day to plant beans   August 9

All of this figuring means that if you plant beans on or before August 9, you should have a harvest of fresh beans before the frost lays them low.

Hardy plants survive that first frost, so just count back from first frost date for them.

Chapter 2

Soil Requirements

Soils are classified by the size of their particles. Generally, they range from coarse to fine or from light to heavy. Here are some basic soil types:

Type	Characteristics
Sandy	Easily tilled
Sandy loam	Well drained; warms quickly
Loam	Poor nutrient retention
Silty loam	Hard to work
Clay loam	Slow drainage; great moisture retention
Clay	Warms slowly; excellent nutrient retention

The coarser the soil, the earlier it warms in the spring and the earlier it can be worked. Coarse particles of sand retain less moisture than fine particles of clay. Coarse soils require less spring sunshine to reach a temperature suitable for seed germination and growth.

Delay working the soil until it is dry enough so that a compressed ball of soil will break apart when dropped from the height of your hip. Soil that is worked when too moist forms compact clods and makes root growth difficult.

Testing Soil pH

The ideal garden soil is rich in organic matter, well drained, slightly acid, and replenished with plant nutrients. How good is your soil? The amount of nutrients and the level of acidity can be determined by soil tests.

These tests are usually performed by your county's Agricultural Extension Service at little or no charge. You can also do your own test, using a kit purchased through the mail or at better garden and hardware stores.

If you use the Extension Service, contact the nearest office and request specific instructions. Check first in the phone book under county government listings for your own or neighboring counties. In general, these are the guidelines many Extension Service offices recommend:

■ Use a trowel to recover small amounts of soil at a depth of about 6 inches.

■ Take several samples from across the garden. Mix these in a bucket to get an accurate indication of average soil conditions in your garden.

■ Avoid collecting soil where peas, beans, or other nitrogen-fixing crops have been grown in previous years.

Dry two or three handfuls of the soil from the bucket at room temperature. Drying with a stove can lead to a false indication of the need for lime. Send a small plastic bag of dry soil to your nearest Extension Service office.

Another tip: Do your soil test in the fall. Extension Service offices are often swamped with requests in the spring, causing delays of up to a month. By having the soil test results on hand early, you will be able to purchase the necessary fertilizers during the winter. That way, you'll be gardening in the first good spring weather, rather than fighting crowds at the local garden-supply store.

The acidity or alkalinity of the soil (the *pH level*) is an important factor in your test. Most plants have a specific pH range within which they thrive and outside of which they perform poorly, if at all. A pH level of 7 represents neutrality, when the soil is neither acid nor alkaline. Levels higher than 7 indicate alkalinity, while numbers below 7 indicate an acid state.

ADJUSTING SOIL pH

Excessive soil acidity is usually corrected by adding lime, in one of three forms: ground limestone (the most commonly used form), burned lime (not recommended), and hydrated lime. The latter two are derived from the first.

You can adjust the pH of your soil, if necessary, by applying lime or other materials as suggested in the table below. Spread the material as evenly as possible and work it into the top 3 or 4 inches of soil uniformly. (If you should need to substitute one form of lime for another: 100 pounds of ground limestone equals 74 pounds of hydrated lime.)

Most fertilizers contain varying amounts of the three essential plant foods: nitrogen (N), phosphorus (P), and potassium (K). On the label of commercial fertilizer bags, the elements are listed in the order given above. A bag of fertilizer listed as 10-15-20, for example, would contain 10 percent nitrogen, 15 percent phosphorus, and 20 percent potassium.

Fertilizers are also available in organic forms, that is, derived from animal, vegetable, or mineral sources. Commercially prepared organic fertilizers tend to be more expensive than chemicals and slower-acting, but they provide a more sustained feeding to the plants and generally improve the soil's condition.

ADJUSTING SOIL pH

TO RAISE SOIL
ONE UNIT OF pH

	HYDRATED LIME	DOLOMITE	GROUND LIMESTONE
Light Soil 100 sq. ft.	1½ pounds	2 pounds	2½ pounds
Heavy Soil 100 sq. ft.	3½ pounds	5½ pounds	6 pounds

TO LOWER SOIL
ONE UNIT OF pH

	SULPHUR	ALUMINUM SULPHATE	IRON SULPHATE
Light Soil 100 sq. ft.	½ pound	2½ pounds	3 pounds
Heavy Soil 100 sq. ft.	2 pounds	6½ pounds	7½ pounds

Chapter 3

Seed Selection

In today's busy world, many of us look for the easiest and quickest way to achieve a goal. Buying plants at the nursery is a fast and simple way to get a garden growing. Why bother starting your own plants from seed? Actually, there are several reasons you might want to do so.

Each year, seed companies introduce new vegetables with more luscious fruit. It's not always possible to find nursery plants of these varieties, and if you want to have them you must grow them from seed.

Growing your own plants from seed is also more economical than buying plants from a nursery, a serious consideration if you have a large garden.

Some plants do well *only* when grown from seed. These include vegetables like beets, carrots, radishes, and peas.

Children may be introduced to gardening by growing their own seedlings. Watching them witness the wonder of "creation" is a reward in itself.

And finally, there is a certain satisfaction, come July, in looking around a thriving garden and knowing that you were responsible for starting these plants from the very beginning.

Climate Limitations

Since climates vary greatly throughout the world, where you live should always be taken into account when you plan your garden. Maximum summer and minimum winter temperatures should be considered, as well as annual rainfall. For best success, try plants recommended for your area, making these your garden standards. This determined, you can then have fun experimenting each year with a few borderline plants, those that do best in either a warmer or colder climate. Often, by providing shelter or otherwise creating your own "microclimate," you can grow these successfully. Some natural feature of your land, such as a pond, may enable you to grow something that your neighbor, a few miles away, cannot. Mulching to keep the ground cool for certain plants may help. Improving the soil with humus often makes it possible to grow vegetables or plants that formerly were unsuccessful in your garden. Winter protection will help in the North, shade or a windbreak in the South.

The following table indicates the sensitivity of certain vegetables to frost and suggests the best planting times for them.

PLANTING DATES IN RELATION TO FROST

HARDY Plant as soon as ground can be prepared.	SEMI-HARDY Plant 1-2 weeks before average date of last frost.	TENDER Plant 1 week after date of last frost.	VERY TENDER Plant 2 weeks after date of last frost.
Asparagus	Cauliflower	New Zealand spinach	Cucumber
Beet	Potato	Snap Bean	Lima Bean
Broccoli		Sweet Corn	Muskmelon
Cabbage		Tomato	Pepper
Carrot			Pumpkin
Kale			Squash
Lettuce			Watermelon
Onion			
Parsnip			
Pea			
Radish			
Spinach			
Swiss Chard			
Turnip			

WHAT TO LOOK FOR

Seeds are available from a number of different sources, and since the federal government has laws regarding purity and germination, any dealer working interstate must meet high minimum standards.

Seed catalogs are fun to browse through, and once you order from one company you will probably receive catalogs from others, as many sell their mailing lists among themselves.

The following list of seed suppliers is not intended as an endorsement or advertisement for these companies. Rather, it is a list of those with interesting catalogs, good reputations, and, by and large, good merchandise.

VEGETABLE SEED SUPPLIERS

Alberta Nursery and Seeds, Ltd., Box 20, Bowden, Alberta, T0M 0K0, Canada.
Hybrid seeds and perennial plants adapted to short-season areas.

Burpee Seed Co., 300 Park Ave., Warminster, PA 18991 (home office); Clinton, IA 52732; Riverside, CA 92502.
The granddaddy of seed companies, with one of the largest selections anywhere.

Comstock, Ferre, & Co., 263 Main Street, Wethersfield, CT 06109.
Catalog of herb, flower, and vegetable seeds.

Gurney's Seed & Nursery Co., Yankton, SD 50079. Vegetable and flower seeds, fruit and nut trees; novelty items, including blue potatoes. Published biannually.

Harris Seeds, 961 Lyell Ave., Rochester, NY 14624. Vegetable and herb seeds.

H.G. Hastings Co., P.O. Box 115535, Atlanta, GA 30310. Vegetable and herb seeds, shrubs, bulbs, berries, and trees for the South.

Le Jardin du Gourmet, West Danville, VT 05873. Herb, vegetable, and flower seeds.

Johnny's Selected Seeds, 305 Foss Hill Rd., Albion, ME 04910. Organically grown seeds of standard vegetable varieties, stressing adaptation to the North.

Kilgore Seed Co., 1400 W. First St., Sanford, FL 32771. Flower, herb, vegetable, and grass seeds adapted to a subtropical climate.

Landreth Seed Co., 180-188 W. Ostend St., Baltimore, MD 21230. George Washington bought seeds from this 194-year-old firm.

Mellinger's Inc., 2340 South Range Road, North Lima, OH 44452. Fruit and nut trees, berries and vines; vegetable, flower, and tree seeds.

Park Seed Co., Box 31, Cokesbury Rd., Greenwood, SC 29647. Features a huge selection of seeds, plants, bulbs, and gardening projects.

Redwood City Seed Co., P.O. Box 361, Redwood City, CA 94064. Catalog of vegetable, nut, fruit, and herb seeds.

Stokes Seeds Inc., Box 548, 737 Main Street, Buffalo, NY 14240. Huge selection of vegetable seeds, with growing tips.

Thompson & Morgan, P.O. Box 1308, Jackson, NJ 08527. European vegetable and flower seeds and unique garden supplies.

Growing Your Own Seeds for Planting

If you raise and save seed, you are producing seed for *your* garden, and, by careful selection over several generations of plants, you can produce plants best suited to *your* climate and *your* garden conditions.

A few seasons ago seeds became scarce as the number of home gardeners spurted. Something like this could happen again in the future, caused by a truck strike, blizzard, postal mix-up, or crop failure. If you have raised and saved seeds, such an event will not hamper your gardening activities one bit. In fact, if you have raised more seeds than you need, you will be able to help your neighbors in a most meaningful way.

If you have a keen eye as you observe, evaluate, select, and compare your plants, you may find something new and valuable. Chances may be against it, but good new strains of plants have been found and are being found — most of them by plant breeders, but a few by observant everyday gardeners. One such person was a turn-of-the-century seed grower, C. N. Keeney of New York State, who is credited with originating nine new varieties of beans, among them Burpee's Stringless Green Pod, still listed in the Burpee catalog and credited as having the "finest in flavor."

There's one benefit of saving seeds on which you yourself will have to put a value. Let's say you first attempt something easy — saving peas. The year that you plant those peas, you will put them in the ground with a little extra care. They'll get the choice compost for encouragement. You'll spend a minute or two longer with them each time you cultivate around them. And, sure enough, they'll taste a bit sweeter than any other peas you raise that year. There'll be a deeper satisfaction in growing them. What's that worth to you?

Chapter 4

Starting Seeds Indoors

There are a number of good reasons to start seeds indoors. Many annuals and vegetables have such a long growing season that they won't flower or fruit if they don't get a head start indoors, especially in the North. Others may not need to be started indoors, but will flower or be productive for a much longer time if started early. Plants with fine seeds should be started indoors to protect them from the ravages of weather. Indoor seed starting eliminates worries about weeds, insects, disease, and excessive heat.

While many vegetables can be sown directly into the garden bed, others must be started indoors, since the growing season, in all but the warmest parts of the country, is not long enough for them to produce. These include broccoli, brussels sprouts, cabbage, cauliflower, celery, eggplant, leeks, okra, peppers, and tomatoes. Lettuce, onions, and melons are often started indoors as well.

Materials You Will Need

You need seeds, of course, and you'll also need a few more supplies to be successful at starting plants from seed.

Containers

Basically, anything that can hold a growing medium and is the right size can be used as a container to germinate seeds. There are many types of containers commercially available that are easy to use and reuse.

Seed-sowing flats should be about 3 to 3½ inches deep and can be of any size, depending on how many seeds you intend to germinate. Generally the ones you buy are made of plastic or fiber. The fiber ones are not as good as the plastic ones, since they cannot be sterilized and therefore should not be reused. They also dry out more quickly. On the other hand, their porosity ensures good aeration, so they do have some advantages.

Peat pots are good for seeds that resent transplanting, and for larger seeds. These pots are round or square, usually 2½ to

3 inches across, and are a combined germinating/growing/transplanting unit. Seeds are sown directly into the pot, and then later the pot is planted along with the plant. Peat pots are also useful for transplanting seedlings sown in flats.

Peat pellets, the most popular being the Jiffy products, are made of compressed peat. When placed in water they expand into a germinating/growing/transplanting unit, similar to the peat pot. They are best for larger, reliably germinating seeds and seeds that resent transplanting.

To keep peat pots and pellets properly watered and protected, place them in a plastic tray or container.

A new germinating method uses what are known as plugs, which are cone- or cylinder-shaped transplants. You can buy plug trays, which may have up to 200 plug holes. The holes are filled with growing medium, and one seed is sown into each plug. The unit goes from germination to transplanting without disturbing the roots.

You can make your own containers from things lying about the kitchen, such as coffee cans, paper cups, aluminum baking trays, milk or juice containers, or plastic food storage containers. Before you use them, wash them well with soap and water and rinse them in a bleach solution (1 ounce or ⅛ cup of bleach per 2 gallons water) to prevent diseases that might kill your seedlings.

Containers have two basic requirements in addition to cleanliness. The container should be 3 to 3½ inches deep for proper root development. Less than that and the roots will not have enough room to grow and will dry out too quickly. Deeper containers waste medium and serve no purpose.

Containers must also have excellent drainage. Purchased containers will already have drainage holes in the bottom. If you make your own containers, be sure to punch out some drainage holes in the bottom.

GERMINATING MEDIA

No one perfect germinating medium exists, but some are better than others. Let's take a look at the components of the various germinating media to decide which is best.

Peat. Baled or bagged peat moss sold in garden centers consists of partially decomposed aquatic plants, and its composition varies greatly. Its pH can range from very acidic to almost neutral. Peat moss has a high water-holding capacity and contains some nitrogen (about 1 percent), one of the elements necessary for plant growth. Peat moss is rarely used by itself for any type of propagating or growing, since water may not penetrate it easily or evenly. Also, it does not have good drainage or aeration qualities by itself. It is, however, a widely used component in sowing and growing mixtures.

Sphagnum Moss. Sphagnum moss is harvested from bogs and dried. It is relatively sterile, lightweight, and able to absorb 10 to 20 times its weight in water. It is generally milled (shredded) for use as a seed-sowing medium. Its fertilizer value is low, so weak fertilizer solutions must be used with it after seedlings emerge. Because it is very acidic (pH 3.5), it can inhibit "damping-off" — a fungal disease that can occur in cold, wet, early spring soils, and that can destroy young seedlings.

For years milled sphagnum moss was recommended as the best germination medium, to be used by itself. Unfortunately, it has some drawbacks — it is very difficult to moisten evenly and it often cakes when it dries out. It has now given way to better mixtures, some of which contain sphagnum moss.

Vermiculite. Vermiculite is expanded mica and it has the capacity to hold tremendous amounts of water for long periods of time. Although it is not usually used alone for seed germination, it is an excellent addition to a soil mixture because it is both light and sterile. Its pH is neutral, it holds nutrients well, provides good aeration, and contains a high percentage of magnesium and potassium, two elements necessary for good root growth.

Perlite. Gray-white perlite is a volcanic ash, which does not absorb water, but holds water on its surface. It contains no essential elements and does not hold nutrients, but it is valuable as a component in a germinating mix because it is light, sterile, and promotes good aeration. Like vermiculite, its pH is neutral.

Perlite stays cool and, therefore, is good in mixes used for germinating seeds that prefer lower temperatures. Its main disadvantage is that it will float to the surface when the seed bed is watered. It comes in various sizes; for seed germinating, use the finest kind.

Sand. Coarse builder's sand is often recommended for rooting plant cuttings, but it is not a good choice for seed sowing. It is heavy, contains no essential elements, does not hold nutrients, and is far from sterile. Stay away from it!

Soil. Soil from the garden should not be used to germinate seeds. It usually doesn't have the right texture to provide proper drainage and aeration, and seedlings may drown in it.

If soil must be used, it should be sterilized to kill the large number of weed seeds, insects, and fungi that may be present in it. Bake in a shallow pan in the oven, holding a temperature of 180° F. for 30 minutes. Use a meat thermometer to make sure the temperature is right. Be prepared! This process emits an unpleasant odor. Commercial growers sterilize soil with chemicals, but this method is not recommended for amateur growers.

Mixtures. The best media for germinating seeds are sterile, soilless mixtures of peat or sphagnum moss with vermiculite and/or perlite. You can make these yourself, using from one-third to one-half sphagnum or peat moss, with the remainder vermiculite or perlite or a combination of the two. Experiment and choose the combination that works best for you.

The easiest way to obtain your germinating medium is to buy it ready-made. Many commercially available mixtures combine peat or sphagnum moss with vermiculite and/or perlite, and add enough fertilizer to get the seedlings off to a good start. This same mix can be used for transplanting and growing in containers.

The "perfect medium" has 50 percent solid material, 25 percent air spaces (in which roots grow and obtain necessary oxygen), and 25 percent moisture. A good mix is light, sterile, and firm but airy. It drains properly, yet retains the right amount of moisture for plant development. It helps eliminate damping-off, reduces the need for constant watching and expert judgment, promotes ideal growth, and lets you grow even the most difficult plants from seeds.

ENVIRONMENTAL CONDITIONS

Germination Temperature. Correct temperature is one of the environmental conditions critical for seed germination. While most seeds require temperatures of 70° F. to 75° F. to germinate, some require cooler temperatures.

Although the temperature in the room of a house may be 70° F., the medium in the germinating flat will be lower because it cools down as the surface moisture evaporates. To keep the medium at 70° F. or above, gentle bottom heat is recommended. This heat may be obtained from a warm spot, such as on top of the refrigerator, or from a heating cable or heating tray.

Heating cables and trays can be spread out wherever seeds are germinated, whether it be on a windowsill or countertop or under fluorescent lights, with the germinating containers placed on top of them. They will heat flats to 70°F. to 75°F. When the flat gets warm enough (add a thermometer to your equipment list), simply pull the plug. Some have a built-in thermostat which automatically turns the system on and off. Waterproof soil-heating cables may also be used in outdoor beds and cold frames.

If seeds are germinated indoors during the heat of summer, room temperatures will probably go high enough so that heating cables and heating trays will not be necessary (unless your house is air conditioned).

When cool temperatures are required, germinate the seeds indoors in an unheated garage, attic, basement, or porch that has some source of natural or artificial light. Outdoors, cool germination temperatures are achieved in early spring or fall. Sow directly into seed beds, or set the flats outside in a spot protected from sun and wind, or in a cold frame.

Moisture and Humidity. Moisture and humidity are also critical for good germination. The germinating medium must be kept evenly moist, but never soaking wet. If there is too little moisture, germination will not occur; too much and the seeds will rot. If a good medium is used, watered thoroughly, and allowed to drain for several hours before sowing, the moisture level should be perfect.

It is best to slip your seed flats into plastic bags or cover them with glass until the seeds germinate. This will keep the level of moisture and humidity just right, so the seed flats will not have to be watered often, if at all, before germination. This will eliminate the problems caused by overwatering, by forgetfulness, or by accidentally dislodging tiny seeds before they germinate.

Light. The final environmental factor, but one as equally important as the others, is light. Some seeds require light to germinate, while others need a complete absence of it to sprout. If light is needed for germination, the solution is not to cover the seeds. If darkness is necessary, cover the seeds completely with medium, unless they are too fine to be covered. In that case, place the seed flats in total darkness or cover them with a material like newspaper or black plastic to block out the light until germination occurs.

Once germinated, all seedlings need ample light to develop into strong, healthy plants. In fact, seedlings have the highest light intensity requirements of all plants. Using fluorescent lights or growing seedlings in a greenhouse is best, but if you do not have these available, an unshaded south window will do almost as well.

Light is necessary to enable plants to convert water and carbon dioxide into sugar (their food) in a process known as *photosynthesis*. If the light intensity if too low, which often happens during the short days of winter or prolonged cloudy periods, the plants will be unhealthy, tall, and spindly.

Other Needs. There are a few other supplies needed to make seed germinating successful. Labels are very important, for no matter how good your memory is, you can't possibly remember which seed is in which flat, or when it was sown. Heavy white plastic markers are widely used, for they are durable and reusable. You can write on them in pencil, and your markings will stay there until you erase or wash them off. Keep them with your plants after you've moved them into the garden, for your own information or in case a friend asks about certain plant or variety. If you have good success with a particular variety, you'll want to know just what it is so you can grow it again.

Young seedlings have to be watered carefully so that they don't become damaged or dislodged. You can either water the plants from the bottom or use a mister.

A record book is a last good "extra." If you keep records this year, you'll appreciate being able to doublecheck next year on what and when you planted, how long it took various seeds to germinate, whether you started them too early or too late, and whether you grew too few or too many of a particular plant.

Hundreds of seedlings can be started using this arrangement and four-foot fluorescent units.

Germination and Care Requirements

Germinating. Once your seed flat is ready, place it in a location where it will receive the proper light and temperature for seed

23

germination. If you have an area in the house, such as a spare room, attic, or basement, where your seed garden would be out of sight and where a water spill or other accident wouldn't cause a problem, so much the better. If not, you can use the kitchen, den, or bedroom — wherever you have the space. If you will be using a windowsill, it's wise to protect it from moisture.

With a few exceptions, seed flats should be placed in good light but not in direct sun or under fluorescent lights while germination is taking place.

The use of a soil thermometer will ensure that the medium is at the right temperature for germination.

Don't give up too early if your seeds don't germinate. If, however, too much time has gone by, try to figure out what went wrong and start again.

Even though the glass or plastic covering the seed flat should minimize the need for watering, check the medium once in a while to make sure it isn't drying out.

Condensation on the plastic or glass does not necessarily mean the flat has been overwatered; a change in temperature may cause moisture to form. Feel the medium to be sure. If it is too wet, leave the glass or plastic off for several hours to dry it a little, and then cover it again. Do not, however, let the medium dry out completely at any time.

Once the seeds have started to germinate, remove the plastic or glass from the seed flats. Gradually move the seedlings into full sun or strong light; sudden changes in light may injure tender seedlings.

Germinating under Lights. If you have the space, germinating seeds under lights is the most productive method. That way, you won't have to worry about short and cloudy days or limited space on windowsills.

You can purchase one of the many fluorescent lights available for indoor gardens, but since seedlings need light in the blue and green area of the spectrum to grow properly (yellow, orange, and red wavelengths promote flowering), you can also use common household cool white lights.

Except for those seeds requiring darkness to germinate, place seedling flats under lights for 24 hours a day until germination occurs. After that, the light duration should be cut down to 12 to 14 hours per day. Once the plants start to grow, the light source should be 3 to 6 inches above the top of the seedlings. To accomplish this, you'll need a system to either raise the lights or lower the shelves as the plants grow.

If the leaves turn downward or look burned during growth, the lights are too close. If the seedlings are starting to grow tall and spindly, the lights are too far away.

Seedling Care. In the following weeks, how you care for your seedlings is critical. Water is the most important consideration. The root systems of the new seedlings are not yet well developed, so the medium must always be kept moist (but never completely wet, or the seedlings will suffer from poor aeration). If the medium starts to lighten in color, that is a sure sign that it is drying out. Check every day to see if water is needed. Watering from the bottom is best until the seedlings reach a fairly good size, since watering from above can dislodge young plants or knock them over. If you do water from above, water the medium between the seedling rows.

Most plants will grow successfully at normal room temperatures of 60° to 70° F. Those that require cooler germination temperatures usually like cooler growing temperatures as well.

If seedlings are grown on the windowsill or at the edge of the light garden, they should be turned regularly so they will grow straight and evenly.

Once the first "true leaves" have developed (the first growth you will see are the *cotyledons,* which are actually food storage cells), it is time to start fertilizing. No food is needed prior to this point, since the seedling is using food that was stored in the seed. Use a soluble plant food such as Hyponex, Miracle-Gro, or Peters at one-quarter the label strength when seedlings are small, increasing to one-half the label strength as the plant matures. It is better to fertilize with this weak solution once a week instead of feeding with a full-strength fertilizer solution once a month;

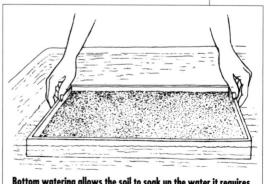
Bottom watering allows the soil to soak up the water it requires.

growth will be more even and "burning" of the seedlings will be avoided. When bottom-watering young seedlings, mix the fertilizer into the water; later on, the seedlings can be fertilized from above.

CHAPTER 5

TRANSPLANTING SEEDLINGS

It is possible to plant seedlings directly from the seed flat into the garden, but this is generally not advised. The seedlings should be transplanted to a larger container first or at least thinned so they will not be crowded, leggy, weak, or susceptible to damage. One transplanting is usually enough; it will guarantee good, strong root development and an easier adjustment of the plant to the garden. Seedlings started in individual pots do not need to be transplanted.

After the seedlings have developed four true leaves, it is time to transplant or thin them. If thinning, leave at least 1 inch between seedlings in the flat. Larger seedlings will need more space. These seedlings may now be left to grow until it is time to transplant them into the garden, although they will benefit from being transplanting at this point into their own pots.

When transplanting, first water the seedlings thoroughly. Peat pots, pellets, or small plastic pots are best for transplanting. If the seedlings are being transplanted into peat pots or flats, wet the containers as well, and don't forget to pre-moisten the medium to be used for transplanting. Seedlings can also be transplanted into flats; those with dividers or compartments lead to more compact root development and easier transplanting, without shock to the roots.

You may use the same medium you used for germinating for transplanting, or use leftover medium from previous seed sowings. It is not critical that the transplanting medium be sterile.

Fill the container with pre-moistened medium to just below the top. With a label or pencil, open a hole in the center of the medium, deep and wide enough to fit the seedling's roots.

Using a white plastic marker, spoon handle, fork, or similar tool, gently lift the seedlings from the flat. Separate them carefully so as not to break any more roots than necessary. A small amount of medium should cling to the seedling's roots. Always handle a seedling by its leaves and NEVER by its stem; if damage is accidentally done, the seedling will grow new leaves, but not a new stem.

Lower the seedling into the hole you made in the medium, placing it slightly deeper than the level at which it was growing in the seed flat. Then gently press the medium around the roots. Don't forget to put a white plastic marker in the container to identify the plant!

Peat pots and pellets should be set into an empty tray or flat to keep them intact and to catch excess water.

Transplants will often droop or wilt because they have lost some of their roots. They will, however, recover quickly if cared for properly. Keep the transplants in good light (but not full sun) for several days, increasing the light intensity gradually. If you've transplanted during cloudy weather, the containers can go right onto the windowsill; if you grow under lights, the transplants can go under the fluorescents right away. Remember that, if the plants become tall and spindly later on, they're probably not getting enough light.

Water when necessary, never allowing the transplants to wilt, and keeping the medium evenly moist but not soaking wet. Once a week, when watering, add soluble fertilizer at one-half the recommended label strength.

Once roots show through the container walls, the plants are ready to be moved to the garden. If it's too early for outdoor planting, they may be held in the container for up to four weeks until weather conditions are favorable for planting.

HARDENING OFF

One week before indoor-grown seedlings are shifted outdoors to the garden, begin to harden them off. This process helps to acclimate the soft and tender plants, letting them gradually get used to their new environment.

Move the trays or flats of potted plants outside into a sheltered, shady area such as a porch, cold frame, or under a tree or shrub. If it gets cold at night, move them back inside. After two or three days, give them half a day of sun, increasing the exposure gradually to a full day. Make sure the transplants are well watered during this "hardening off" period. If at all possible, don't place transplants on the ground if slugs are a problem in your area.

MOVING INTO THE GARDEN

Doublecheck planting dates before you start moving plants outside. Most vegetables must wait until all danger of frost has passed to be placed outside; a few can go out earlier. Tomatoes, eggplant, and peppers should wait a little longer still, until the ground has warmed up completely. See the map on page 77 to find the mean last frost date for your area. (**Note:** In some areas, local frost conditions can vary widely. Contact your county Agricultural Extension Service for specific information.)

Before moving plants into the garden, water both the ground outside and the transplants. This will cut down on transplanting shock. Try to do your transplanting on a cloudy day or late in the afternoon, so that the heat of the sun won't cause excessive wilting. If you've used individual peat pots or peat pellets, transplant shock and wilting will be minimal.

Dig a hole about twice the size of the root ball. Set the transplant into the hole so the root ball will be covered by ¼ inch of soil, and press the soil firmly around the plant's roots, so there is good contact between the soil and the roots.

Seedlings in peat pellets can be planted as they are. When planting a peat pot, peel whatever you can off the pot before planting, so that the walls of the pot will not confine the roots. Be sure the peat pot is completely covered with soil; otherwise it will act like a wick to dry out the plant, allowing moisture to escape from around the roots.

If your transplants have been growing in flats that are not compartmentalized, very carefully cut out a root ball with a knife or trowel. If the transplants have been growing in individual plastic pots or flat compartments, turn them upside down and tap them on the bottom, and they should come out easily.

The newly set-out plants may look a little sparse at first, but they will grow and fill in quickly, and you won't want them to be overcrowded. Adequate spacing also improves air circulation and cuts down on disease.

Water plants well immediately after transplanting and again every day for about a week, until the plants are well established and growing. Some transplants may wilt at first, but misting them every day or shading them will help them revive quickly.

Frost Protection

If an unexpected late frost occurs after transplanting, you will need to protect your tender seedlings from frost damage. This can be done by placing Styrofoam cups or plastic milk jugs over the plants when frost threatens and removing them when the temperature warms up.

Chapter 6

Wide-Row Planting

What Are the Advantages?

Wide-row gardening is an eye-opening experience for many folks. They find they need less space and need to work fewer hours to raise more and better vegetables, even when weather conditions are less than ideal.

Wide-row gardening means planting vegetables in bands that are 10, 12, 14, or more inches in width, and any length. Instead of a single file of plants, one right after the other, you'll have a solid bed of plants, each just inches away from its nearest neighbor.

And now for the advantages:

■ More garden area is used for plants, less for walkways. Thus, you'll be able to produce more in the same amount of space.

■ Less time is spent planting seeds.

■ Less weeding is involved. The crops themselves form a living mulch.

■ Moisture is conserved. Plants shade the soil, so it dries out more slowly.

■ In midsummer, the crops shade and cool the soil.

■ Harvesting is easier. You can pick a lot without moving up and down a row.

■ The harvesting period is longer.

■ There's less soil compaction close to plants, so the plants grow better.

Preparing the Soil

Good soil preparation can help you get more out of any garden, but when you use wide rows, it can be especially rewarding. Planting, thinning, cultivating, and every other operation related to wide rows is much easier when you have a loose, loamy soil that's rich in organic matter. Good soil will also ensure healthier, more nutritious, and more productive crops.

Unfortunately, few people are blessed with ideal soil to start with. Some have clay, some have sand, and some seem to grow an abundant crop of stones. But, with the right preparation, you can garden successfully on any of these soil types and plant wide rows on all of them.

If you can get your hands on any sort of organic matter, you should add it to your soil. Use grass clippings, compost, leaves, spoiled hay, weed-free manure, or any other kind of dead or decaying vegetable matter. Till or spade the organic matter into the soil to a depth of 4 to 6 inches. Be sure to do this early enough in the season, so that the materials are well-decayed before planting time. In fact, it is often best to add organic matter the previous fall.

Before planting, you should have your soil broken up to the point where it is loose and crumbly. When soil reaches this condition, is said to have "good tilth." You can work the soil by hand, but renting or borrowing some sort of power equipment will save you lots of sweat and possibly a sore back. A rototiller with tines in the rear is the ideal tool for soil preparation. It leaves a smooth seedbed that requires little, if any, raking.

NOTE: Once you have worked up the soil, be careful not to walk on any of the areas where you will be planting seeds. This is important if you want the best possible results with your wide rows.

Planting and Weeding a Wide Row

Start with a loose, fertile seedbed. Garden soil is loaded with weed seeds, but only those near the surface will germinate. Working the soil moves weed seeds to the germination zone, where they will sprout. Work the soil over several times. Many weed seeds will germinate, leaving fewer to trouble you later on.

How to Plant a Wide Row

1. Mark the edge of the row with string. Be sure not to walk in the row; work from one side of it.

2. Mark the width of the row by drawing a garden rake alongside the string. The width of the rake — about 16 inches — is ideal. Dragging the rake down the wide row also removes debris and smooths and levels the seedbed.

3. Fertilize the row area, if necessary. Use 2 cups of commercial fertilizer such as 5-10-10 for every 10 feet of row, or 4 cups

of dehydrated manure. Add high-phosphorus fertilizer, such as bonemeal, for root crops and onions. Rake in the fertilizer, then smooth the soil with the back of a rake.

4. Broadcast the seeds, sprinkling them evenly over the length and width of the row like grass seed. Don't worry too much about spacing, but it's better to sow too thickly; plants can be thinned easily later on. Here are two planting tips: Sprinkle in a few radish seeds with whatever you're planting. Radishes make good companion plants. First of all, they'll germinate and mark the wide row. Then, as you harvest them, they will loosen the soil. Large seeds are easy to space correctly, but small seeds can be tricky. Try using a discarded spice shaker bottle, such as the one used for garlic powder. It makes a great wide-row seeder.

5. Firm the seeds down gently with the back of a hoe or rake.

6. Cover the seeds with soil to a depth equal to four times their diameter. That's about 1 inch for large seeds such as peas and beans, ¼ inch for small ones such as lettuce and carrots. Pull soil from beyond the row, lift it into the center of the seedbed, and then, using the back of a rake, level it over the seeds.

7. Tamp down the seedbed with a hoe or rake, so that the seeds make good contact with the soil.

Until the seedlings come up, keep the seedbed moist. If a crust forms on claylike soil, drag a rake gently over the top to break up the crust.

Thinning and Weeding

Many people think that thinning a wide row is difficult, but it is actually one of the simplest operations. First of all, vegetables that have large seeds, or those that need to be transplanted into the garden should be properly spaced when planted and should not need to be thinned. Most of the crops in the "small seed" category, however, *will* need to be thinned as soon as they come up. This can be done quickly and easily with an ordinary garden rake. Just drag it across the row so that the teeth dig into the soil at a depth of about ¼ to ½ inch. Don't press down too much, though, or the teeth will dig in too deeply. One thinning should be all you need to do with the rake.

It is very important to do this thinning when the plants are still very small. It may look like a terrible mess at first, but in a few days it will look just fine again and you will have saved yourself countless hours of tedious hand-thinning. At the same time, you will have completed your first weeding and cultivation of the row.

After a week or two, your plants will get too large to drag a rake over them, but they'll still need cultivation. You'll also need some way to cultivate large-seeded crops such as peas and beans. To accomplish this, use a tool called an In-Row-Weeder, a special kind of rake with long, flexible tines. It is designed so that you can drag it right over a row of established plants without injuring them, yet at the same time it will cultivate the soil and kill all the tiny, sprouting weeds.

The important thing is to get the weeds while they are still very tiny. Once they get too large, you will be forced to do a lot of hand-weeding. Don't wait until you see the weeds before you start cultivating within the wide rows.

BEST AND WORST CANDIDATES FOR WIDE-ROW PLANTING

Here are just some of the crops that grow particularly well in wide rows. You may want to try others.

Beans	Mustard
Beets	Onions
Cabbage	Parsnips
Carrots	Peas
Cauliflower	Peppers
Collards	Radishes
Endive	Rutabagas
Kale	Spinach
Kohlrabi	Swiss Chard
Lettuce	Turnips

And here are the vegetables that don't grow as well using the wide-row method.

Corn	Potatoes
Cucumbers	Squash
Melons	Tomatoes

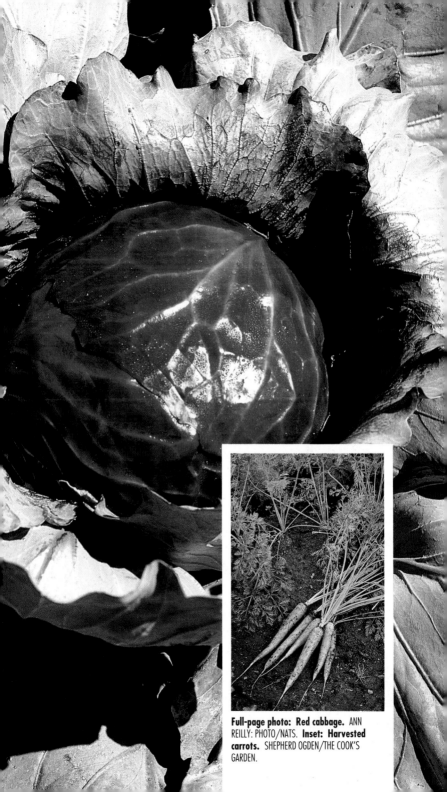

Full-page photo: Red cabbage. ANN REILLY: PHOTO/NATS. **Inset: Harvested carrots.** SHEPHERD OGDEN/THE COOK'S GARDEN.

Full-page photo: A mixed basket of summer squash, featuring (clockwise from bottom) green zucchini and 'Ronde de Nice' and yellow patty pan, straightneck, and crookneck varieties. SHEPHERD OGDEN/THE COOK'S GARDEN. **Inset: 'Spirit' pumpkin.** ANN REILLY: PHOTO/NATS.

Full-page photo: 'Long Red Cayenne' pepper. ANN REILLY: PHOTO/NATS. **Inset, above: Harvested potatoes.** LEE LANDAU: PHOTO/NATS. **Inset, opposite page: 'Kentucky Wonder' pole beans growing on suspended strings.** ANN REILLY: PHOTO/NATS.

Full-page photo: Harvested leeks. SHEPHERD OGDEN/THE COOK'S GARDEN. Inset, opposite page: 'Charentais' and 'Jenny Lind' melons. SHEPHERD OGDEN/THE COOK'S GARDEN. Inset, above: Onions and lettuce growing in raised beds. PRISCILLA CONNELL: PHOTO/NATS.

Full-page photo: 'Sweet 100' cherry tomatoes. ANN REILLY: PHOTO/NATS. **Inset: Tomato plants started from seed.** JEAN BAXTER: PHOTO/NATS.

CHAPTER 7

USING RAISED BEDS

WHAT ARE THE ADVANTAGES?

Raised beds are the gardener's greatest problem-solver.

Do you have heavy clay soil that takes weeks to dry out in the spring? Form raised beds in the fall and you won't waste all that warm weather that's so good for just-planted gardens. Low-lying areas? Their extra moisture can be a plus if it surrounds raised beds. Eager for warm soil in the spring, to plant melons, lima beans, and other heat-loving plants? Raised beds heat up more quickly than flat areas of soil. And dry out much more quickly after sudden downpours that might wash the seeds from conventional plantings. Rainwater doesn't puddle on top of raised beds, either.

These beds are also good in gardens that have a very thin layer of topsoil, effectively doubling the amount available to the plants and making it possible to raise fine root crops.

Working around raised beds is a delight. You don't have to bend over so far to seed or weed or harvest from them, and maintaining them is light work with a hoe.

PREPARING THE SOIL

Once you have the knack of it, making raised beds is a snap. Here are two methods, one using hand tools, the other using a rear-end tiller.

USING HAND TOOLS

1. Prepare a deep, loose seedbed. If it's needed, add compost or fertilizer, or both, to the bed, and mix it into the top few inches of soil.

2. Mark the bed with stakes and strings. The size is up to you; for the first trial, you might mark out a bed that would be about 16 inches wide, so space the strings about 36 inches apart. The top of the bed can be elevated 6 to 10 inches above the walkway, and the bed walls will slope toward the walkway. Experiment to get dimensions with which you feel comfortable.

3. Pull soil from the walkway to the top of the bed. Using a garden rake, move along one walkway, pulling 4 to 6 inches of soil from the opposite walkway. Repeat the process from the other side. Make a pile of the soil. Pile it high — the deeper, the better.

4. Level off the top of the bed, using the back of the rake.

5. Plant the seeds, using steps 4 through 7 under "How to Plant a Wide Row" in Chapter 6.

Using a Tiller

1. Prepare a deep, loose seedbed. Add fertilizer or compost if needed.

2. Stake out the tiller route to form walkways. Set stakes at each end of the row two tiller widths apart.

3. Attach a furrowing and hilling attachment to the tiller. Set the hilling wings to the highest position, so that they'll push a lot of soil upward onto the bed.

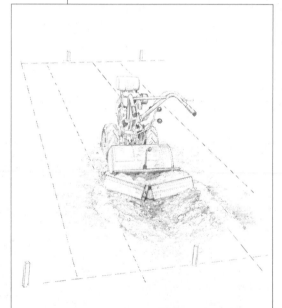

4. Hill up the beds. Line up the center of tiller in front of the first stake, point it at stake at other end of the bed, and guide the tiller directly toward it. Repeat with the next two stakes from the other end of the garden.

5. Smooth the top of the bed with a rake.

6. Plant the seeds, using steps 4 through 7 under "How to Plant a Wide Row" in Chapter 6.

Set stakes two tiller widths apart. Attach furrowing and hilling attachment to tiller. Line up center of the tiller in front of one stake, then till toward the other stake. Continue this to form beds and walkways.

Chapter 8
MULCHING AND FERTILIZING

An excellent low-cost method of improving your soil is to mulch the garden.

A mulch is a layer of material spread on the surface of the soil to retain moisture and retard weed growth. Until recently, all mulching materials were organic in nature, but plastic mulch has recently come into favor among some growers. The opacity of black plastic mulch makes it the most effective choice for checking weeds and conserving moisture, but it obviously adds nothing to the soil.

Organic mulches are not as fast-acting as manure or other organic fertilizers in enriching the garden, but they are nonetheless good soil builders.

Mulch helps protect the soil from temperature extremes, keeping the ground warmer in the winter and cooler in the summer. It also greatly cuts down on the need to weed and water the garden. Mulch prevents sprawling plants like cucumbers and tomatoes from coming in contact with bare ground, precluding many rot and fungus problems. And soil erosion from wind or water is minimized in a mulched garden.

MULCH MATERIALS

The following list contains mulching materials that you can probably find available for free close to your home,

Leaves	Straw
Leaf mold	Rotten wood
Pine needles	Hulls or shells
Sawdust	Corn cobs or stalks
Seaweed	Newspaper
Spoiled hay	Wood chips or
Scrap material	shavings

At the end of the growing season, most gardeners who use mulch turn the protective covering into the soil, where the action of water and microbes can start the process of making the organic material available as plant food.

Other gardeners leave the mulch in place year after year, replenishing the protective covering as it starts to decay on the soil surface. This is the closest imitation of natural fertilization that the home gardener can undertake, and, after a period of a few years, it will yield noticeable benefits. A single disadvantage is that mulched soils are very slow to warm up in the spring.

35

The mulch, of course, can be pulled away, then put back in place when the crops begin to grow.

FERTILIZER POSSIBILITIES

If your garden soil tests show shortages of nutrients, you can eliminate those shortages through the application of organic fertilizers.

PROS AND CONS OF COMMON MULCHES

MATERIAL	PRO	CON
Straw/Hay	Cheap; generally available; adds organic matter.	Can contain weed seeds, insects and/or disease.
Leaves	Readily available; generally free; rich in nutrients.	Can mat down or be too acidic for some plants.
Grass clippings	Easy to get and apply; good source of nitrogen.	Can burn plants; may contain weed seeds.
Pine needles	Attractive; easy to apply.	Large quantities hard to collect; may be to acidic.
Wood shavings	Weed-and disease-free; easy to apply; available.	Can be acidic; tends to tie up nitrogen in the soil.
Manure	Great source of fertility and organic matter.	Should be well-rotted; expensive to buy; usually contains weeds.
Newspaper	Easy to get and apply; earthworms thrive in it.	Decomposes very fast, must be weighted down.
Plastic	Total weed control if opaque kind (black or green) is used; warms soil for early start; heavy-duty plastic can be used for more than one season.	Expensive, unattractive; adds nothing to the soil; must be weighted down and cleaned up in the fall.

Manures, while they vary greatly in the percentages of nutrients they provide, all have one thing in common — application of them will overcome those shortages — and improve your soil in other ways as well. Manures range from the relatively rich (or "hot") 2.5-1.4-0.6 content of rabbit manure to the "cold" 0.5-0.3-0.5 of pig manure.

Manure should be applied much more heavily than is the practice of most gardeners. One hundred pounds of cow manure per 100 square feet of garden space is about right; use half this amount if spreading the "hot" chicken manure and litter.

WHEN AND HOW MUCH TO SIDE-DRESS

VEGETABLE	WHEN TO APPLY	AMOUNT OF COMPLETE FERTILIZER
Broccoli	As heads begin to form	1-2 tablespoons per plant
Brussels Sprouts	When sprouts are size of marbles	1 tablespoon per plant
Cabbage	When heads start to form	1 tablespoon per plant
Cauliflower	When leaves reach maximum size	1-2 tablespoons per plant
Chard	After first harvest	1 tablespoon per foot of 16-inch wide row
Corn	Twice, when 10 inches high and when it starts to tassle	1 tablespoon per plant each time
Cucumbers, Melons & Winter Squash	Before vines start to run	1 tablespoon per plant
Eggplant	When blossoms form	1 tablespoon per plant
Leeks	When 8-12 inches tall	2-3 handfuls of compost mounded around each plant
Onions	When 6-8 inches tall, and every two weeks after until bulbs start to expand	2-3 cups per 10 feet of wide row
Peppers	Blossom time	1 teaspoon (and no more)
Pole Beans	In South only, a week after first picking, then every 3-4 weeks	1 teaspoon per plant
Potatoes	6-7 weeks after planting	1 tablespoon per plant, before hilling
Summer Squash	When buds form	1-2 tablespoons per plant
Tomatoes	First blossoms	1-2 tablespoons per plant

Instead of one tablespoon of a complete fertilizer such as 5-10-10, you can substitute two handfuls good compost, two handfuls dehydrated manure, or one to two tablespoons alfalfa meal.

SIDE DRESSING

Many crops have big appetites, and, if they're to produce their best, they need a midseason snack.

Gardeners call it *side-dressing*. That means adding fertilizer — either commercial or natural — to the soil. It can be done in several ways.

Banding. Great with single-row crops like corn. Make a shallow furrow with a hoe 6 inches to one side of the row. Drop in a thin band of fertilizer, then hoe soil over it.

Circling. Spoon-feed tomatoes, peppers, and other transplanted crops. Use a hoe or trowel to make a circle around each plant 6 inches away from the stem. Spoon in the fertilizer, just a teaspoon per plant, then cover the fertilizer with soil.

Top-Dressing. For wide rows. Sprinkle natural fertilizers — bone-meal, alfalfa meal, compost, etc. — over the row. Don't use commercial fertilizers. They will stick to the plants and burn them.

CHAPTER 9

HARVESTING AND STORAGE

PICK EARLY — PICK OFTEN

Get them while they're little! This time we mean crops, not weeds. It's not only less work to pick young crops; they just plain taste better than tough, overmature produce. Regular picking encourages a plant to produce more, so you'll enjoy a better harvest. Small, tender vegetables also take less time and energy to process. Keep the joy in gardening — never give growing time to a stringy bean, a seedy cucumber or zucchini, starchy peas or corn, a woody beet, bitter lettuce, or tough spinach.

STORING YOUR CROPS

To lower your food costs or save what could be wasted garden surplus, try storing food the natural way, in storage rooms and cellars, or even in the garden.

Storage requires less work and is cheaper and far more energy-efficient than either canning or freezing. And, for many fruits and vegetables, it's the best way to keep them as close as possible to their just-picked or just-dug peak of quality. It's not difficult, either, if you follow a few simple rules.

One of those rules is that crops are particular about where you store them. They want just the right humidity and temperature. You probably have ideal conditions for some of them in your home right now, and, with a little effort, you can provide satisfactory conditions for the others.

Onions like cool, dry conditions. If you have an attic or an unheated room, you have a good place for onions. The closer to the freezing point the temperature goes, the longer your onions will keep.

Warm and dry conditions are favorable for squash, pumpkins, and sweet potatoes. Many of today's homes have cellars that are suitable. The furnace keeps the temperature in the 50° to 55° F. range even during the coldest nights of winter. And the humidity is low. Add a few wooden racks to keep the produce off the concrete floor, and you have a good storage space for these crops.

Potatoes can be stored in well-ventilated boxes at temperatures between 40° and 50°F. Root crops like carrots, parsnips, and beets should be cured in the sun for a day or two after harvesting, then stored in boxes, alternating layers of vegetables with heavy layers of sand. (Beets generally don't keep as long as carrots, so they should be used quickly.) For cabbages, cut off the root and outer leaves and wrap the heads in several layers of newspaper, or hang them up by the roots in a shed or garage.

Another rule to remember is that the maximum storage time for vegetables and fruits varies enormously. Ripe tomatoes and peppers can be held for only a few weeks, whereas winter squash will last through the winter, and dried peas and beans can be stored for several years. None should be stored and forgotten, though. They must be checked often (once a week is not too frequent), to make sure that conditions are as ideal as possible, and to remove any produce that is showing signs of decay.

A third general rule is that you should plan your gardening so that your storage crops reach maturity — no more and no less — just when you wish to store them, which in most cases is before the truly hard frosts that signal the approach of winter. Most of the crops require only drying in the sun for several days before being stored. They should not be washed before being stored, although dried dirt can be brushed off of them. Vegetables for storage should be handled carefully at all times, so that bruises will not invite speedy decay.

TIPS TO REMEMBER WHEN HARVESTING CROPS FOR STORAGE

■ Vegetables to be stored should be left in the garden as long as possible without danger of freezing.

■ Only sound, top-quality produce should be stored. Because of the fast spread of decay organisms, any injured vegetables should be set aside and used first.

■ Handle crops reserved for storage carefully to avoid bruising or the slightest scratch or scrape. Squash and pumpkins, for example, should be handled "like eggs."

■ Mature, hard-ripe vegetables store the longest. Green garden crops should not be stored. (Green tomatoes are the exception. Store them between layers of newspaper or with a few apples to promote ripening.)

■ Vegetables that are the right size and maturity for storage come mostly from summer sowing. Large beets, carrots, etc., sown in the spring are too large and woody for top-quality storage; these should be used in midsummer for table use and canning.

■ When harvesting root crops, use a digging fork to avoid injury to the roots. Always cut off the tops of root vegetables — but never closer than ½ inch to the crown — as soon as you remove them from the soil. Considerable moisture is lost from roots through the leaves if the leaves are left on, and this can cause shriveling of the roots.

■ Vegetables for storage should not be washed. Use a soft brush to remove any soil clinging to roots. All should be stored with a dry surface. (Celery and similar crops should have moisture around the roots, but the foliage must be dry to avoid rot.)

■ Shriveling in vegetables needing moist conditions (beets, carrots, and parsnips) can be prevented by sprinkling the walls and floor of your storage area with water as needed during the winter. Pans of water may also be set out in the storage area.

■ Wooden apple boxes, if used indoors for storage, should be stacked with furring strips between the boxes and the floor to permit full air circulation. Orange crates, mesh bags, and discarded nylon hose are excellent for onion storage.

■ Fruits should never be stored with potatoes, turnips, or cabbage. Gases released from apples in respiration can sprout potatoes; cabbage and turnips transmit their odors to pears and apples.

When storing beets, leave a half-inch of stems so the beets won't bleed.

Chapter 10

Coping with Garden Pests

When dealing with garden pests, the proverbial ounce of prevention is worth a pound of cure. Once the woodchuck has chomped off your beans at ground level, the raccoon has stripped and devoured every ear of corn, and the cucumber beetles have decimated emerging seedlings, you may as well throw up your hands in surrender and hightail it to the nearest farmer's market with your wallet in hand.

If you're in a country place where the woodchuck and rabbit populations are high, **you need a fence**. Invest some time and effort to construct one that's burrow-proof. Build it in the fall, while the memory of crops unsavored (because the varmints got there first) still stings.

CANOPIES OF NYLON NETTING AND OTHER MATERIALS can control a variety of problems — from hungry birds to cabbage worms. Cucumber beetles can be outwitted by tight-fitting cheesecloth,

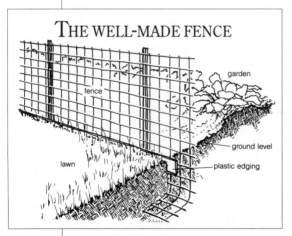

THE WELL-MADE FENCE

garden

fence

ground level

lawn

plastic edging

a nylon net, or a plastic netting frame placed over cucumbers, melons, and squash. Raise the nets as plants grow. Try similar canopies over cauliflower, broccoli, and cabbage beds to prevent cabbage butterflies from laying egg clusters. Nylon netting also can be spread over newly-seeded areas as protection against marauding birds and can even be used to protect onions, radishes, turnips, etc., from flies that deposit eggs of root maggots.

LIZARDS AND SNAKES — the rubber toy variety available in dime stores—spook birds who might otherwise go after your lettuce,

Swiss chard, beets, etc. Place decoys in the open, perhaps on a board, so they're highly visible to birds approaching the area.

MOTHBALLS are said to repel rabbits and bugs, but don't spread them on the soil. Hang small mesh bags of mothballs on trellises or fences, where beans, cucumbers, etc., are growing — or put mothballs in jar lids or similar shallow containers and place on the ground. (Don't do this if your children are likely to get into them.)

WOODCHUCK OR GROUNDHOG DAMAGE. Fencing won't keep woodchucks out, as they're excellent climbers. The best bet for dealing with them is to find their burrow (a new one typically is made each year and most have only one entrance): put several tablespoons of carbon disulfide (readily available in drug stores) on a rag; stuff the treated rag at least a foot into the burrow with a stick; then cover the hole quickly with a rock or log and some soil. Killing gas will form quickly.

Try sprinkling black pepper to discourage hungry rabbits.

RABBITS NIBBLING DOWN YOUR ROWS? Your surest safeguard is a 30-inch fence of 1½ inch mesh sunk 6 inches underground (24 inches above ground). Powdered rock phosphate, flour, or talcum powder sprinkled on the foliage of beans, tomato seedlings, etc., works for many gardeners. Success has also been reported with dried blood meal sprinkled on the soil around plants (never apply directly to the foliage). Reapply after a rain. Rabbits apparently panic at the odor. Marigolds planted around the garden *strictly* as rabbit deterrents are not recommended, since many rabbits love to munch marigolds.

RACCOONS RAIDING YOUR CORN? Nothing seems to be absolutely foolproof, but gardeners have reported varying degrees of success with these "coon chasers":

1. Electric fencing is one of the best deterrents. The first strand should be 6 inches above the soil; the second about 15 inches.

2. Leave a transistor radio on all night (protected by a plastic bag). Talk shows and rock and roll stations work best.

3. Floodlight the garden during key corn ripening periods — flick the light on and off every now and then. Some gardeners place several blinking lanterns around the corn patch; others string up blinking outdoor Christmas lights around the borders.

4. Keep a brave dog tied nearby. Ideally a coon dog.

5. Grow pickling cucumbers, pumpkins, watermelon, or winter squash as a living "fence" around perimeters. A coon likes to see around him and he may not want to enter the vine jungle. *Avoid gaps or he'll slip through.* Once he's had a taste of corn, nothing will keep him away!

6. Grow at least a double row of a very late variety as a protective border around early sweet corn. Coons will wait for the late variety to ripen (while you sneak in and harvest the early corn).

7. Install a 3- to 4-foot fence of chicken wire with a loose overhang of wire projecting above. The overhang needs to be about 1½ to 2 feet. The coon's weight keeps him from climbing such a floppy arrangement.

8. Sprinkle cayenne pepper on corn ears and lime around garden borders.

9. Place dog droppings between the corn plants (not between the rows). Animal odors will sometimes frighten away a raccoon.

10. Walk barefoot around your garden borders at dusk.

11. Never put off harvesting corn that's ready "until tomorrow." Raccoons will invariably visit that very night!

MOLES OR GOPHERS A PROBLEM? To determine active tunnels, stamp all of them flat. Ones that reappear the next day are active. Check into commercially-available traps of various kinds or try these ideas:

1. Soak a Kleenex or rag in peanut or olive oil and push it into gopher or mole runways. The oil quickly becomes rancid and stinks 'em out.

2. Using the same principle, one gardener who had tried "everything else" finally got rid of moles with the help of two large dogs. Mole tunnels were dug open regularly and dog droppings dropped in. Moles took up residence elsewhere.

3. Vibration vexes moles. Stick a child's pinwheel in several spots around the garden if moles are a problem. A larger mole windmill ("Klippety-Klop") designed for this purpose is specifically available at garden centers (or write to Lakeland Nurseries Sales, Hanover, PA 17331).

WIRE COVERS made from 3-foot wire fencing with 2 x 4-inch mesh and shaped into a tent are portable and can be used to keep birds away from peas, lettuce, strawberries, and other crops. Covered at night with plastic, burlap, or newspaper, they can double as frost protection or as cold frames. If available, substitute metal corn crib ventilators.

SLUGS A PROBLEM? Set out shallow pans or wide-mouthed jar tops of stale beer at ground level around the garden at night (but not where cats are apt to spot them, or they'll lap it up). Slugs and snails love beer (they're after the yeast); they drown by the droves. One teaspoon dried yeast mixed with 3 ounces of water may be substituted. If your slugs and snails are teetotalers, try setting out grapefruit rinds (replacing them after two to three days). Sprinkle lime or wood ashes along garden rows, or sprinkle slugs or snails with salt when you spot them. If your garden is surrounded by lawn, try laying down a barrier of sharp sand, diatomaceous earth, or cinders to keep out slugs. Oak leaf mulches apparently provide a "bitter atmosphere," which slugs can't stand. A large cabbage leaf inverted on the ground makes a good trap, as do boards. If coal ashes are available, line garden paths with them. The texture of coal ashes discourages slugs (they can't abide dry, powdery or sharp, prickly surfaces); when the ashes decompose, they release sulfer, which — combined with water — forms sulfuric acid (lethal to slugs). Powdered rock phosphate will deter slugs, plus enrich your soil. Also encourage toads in your garden — they find slugs a tasty treat.

"MIX UP" YOUR PLANTINGS to confuse bugs, planting partial rows of crops at different locations. Concentrations of one type of planting attract pests that attack that crop. Also try interplanting marigolds and herbs, with your vegetables. (Refer to the companion planting chart on pages 8-9.)

INSECT-DETERRING PLANTS

ASTER	Most insects
BASIL	Repels flies and mosquitoes
BORAGE	Deters tomato worm — improves growth and flavor of tomatoes
CALENDULA	Most insects
CATNIP	Deters flea beetle
CELERY	White cabbage butterfly
CHRYSANTHEMUM	Deters most insects
DEAD NETTLE	Deters potato bug — improves growth and flavor of potatoes
EGGPLANT	Deters Colorado potato beetle
FLAX	Deters potato bug
GARLIC	Deters Japanese beetle, other insects, and blight
GERANIUM	Most insects
HENBIT	General insect repellent
HORSERADISH	Plant at corners of potato patch to deter potato bug
HYSSOP	Deters cabbage moth
MARIGOLD	Plant throughout garden to discourage Mexican bean beetles, nematodes, and other insects
MINT	Deters white cabbage moth and ants
MOLE PLANT	Deters moles and mice if planted here and there
NASTURTIUM	Deters aphids, squash bugs, striped pumpkin beetles
ONION FAMILY	Deters most pests
PEPPERMINT	Planted among cabbages, it repels white cabbage butterfly
PETUNIA	Protects beans
RADISH	Especially deters cucumber beetle
ROSEMARY	Deters cabbage moth, bean beetle, and carrot fly
RUE	Deters Japanese beetle
SAGE	Deters cabbage moth, carrot fly
SALSIFY	Repels carrot fly
SOUTHERNWOOD	Deters cabbage moth
SUMMER SAVORY	Deters bean beetles
TANSY	Deters flying insects, Japanese beetles, striped cucumber beetles, squash bugs, ants
THYME	Deters cabbage worm
TOMATO	Asparagus beetle
WORMWOOD	Carrot fly, white cabbage butterfly, black flea beetle

Chapter 11

25 Garden Favorites

Beans

Snap Beans, Bush and Pole

A favorite gardening crop that's easy to grow, productive, can be grown throughout the United States, and does well in almost any soil but a wet one. Bush beans are an excellent wide-row crop and grow well in narrow rows and on raised beds, too. Plant any time from just after the last spring frost to six or seven weeks before the expected first frost. Bush beans grow 15 to 20 inches tall, pole beans as high as 15 feet, but harvesting becomes difficult at that height, so 6 to 8 feet is much more convenient. Some gardeners prefer pole beans because they can raise more in less space, the harvesting season is longer, and many varieties have a delicious, nutlike flavor.

PLANTING: For a wide row of bush beans, broadcast beans 3 to 6 inches apart. Using a rake, pull up soil from beyond the wide row and cover seeds with a 1-inch layer. Tamp the seedbed down gently with the back of a hoe. For narrow rows, sow beans 2 to 4 inches apart, and thin to 4 to 6 inches apart. For pole beans, try tying three or four 8-foot poles together at the top, and set them up tepee style. Plant five or six seeds per pole, and thin to four plants. Or set up two poles about 8 feet apart, link them at the top and bottom with a wire or rope, then dangle strings down from the wire or rope for the beans to climb. Plant beans about 6 inches apart. Winds will test the strength of these poles, so make them strong and firmly implant them. In all cases, treat bean seeds with an organic, nitrogen-fixing legume inoculant (available from most seed suppliers) before planting.

CULTIVATION: Avoid cultivating after a rain or when dew is on the plants, to keep from spreading disease. Hoe gently, to avoid harming roots. Add mulch when the plants are up and the soil is warm.

HARVESTING: Stay out of the garden when the plants are wet. Picking early and often increases the harvest.

ENEMIES: The Mexican bean beetle, tan with eight black spots on each wing, is larger than a ladybug. Hand-pick these beetles, to prevent them from laying egg clusters on the undersides of leaves. Rotenone is also used for beetle control.

VARIETIES: Green bush beans include Improved Tendergreen (56 days to harvest; meaty, dark green, stringless, mosaic-resistant) and Tendercrop (53 days; smooth, round, green pods; mosaic-resistant). Yellow varieties include Brittle Wax (52 days; heavy yields) and Pencil Pod Wax (54 days; hardy, a heavy yielder; good for late fall or early spring plantings). Pole varieties recommended include Kentucky Wonder (65 days) and Blue Lake (60 days).

SUGGESTION: Bush beans are good succession crops to follow peas and early spinach.

Shell Beans, Bush and Pole

Grown for shelling from pods, then eaten green, or allowed to dry on the vine before shelling. There are dozens of varieties, many native to America. These and other bean types are doubly valuable to the gardener, since they enrich the soil with nitrogen. Beans are good to plant where some "hungry" crop, such as corn, grew the previous year. Four ounces of seed will yield 8 pounds of shelled beans. Bush shell beans are great for wide rows and raised beds, where 4 ounces will seed 10 to 15 feet.

PLANTING AND CULTIVATION: See instructions, under Snap Beans, Bush and Pole.

HARVESTING: Leave shell beans are left on the plants until the pods are mature and the beans fill out the pods. Shell beans for immediate eating (or freezing or canning) should be picked when beans can be seen in the pods, but before the pod has passed the growth stage and begun to dry. For dry beans, pods can be allowed to dry on the plant, or mature plants can be cut and stacked to dry, then beans picked or threshed off them.

Let pods get brittle-dry before attempting to shell them.

ENEMIES: See listing under Snap Beans, Bush and Pole.

VARIETIES: The hundreds of varieties of beans make selection an adventure. Choose beans popular in your area, since they must

Full-page photo: 'Melody' spinach. ROBERT E. LYONS: PHOTO/NATS.
Inset: Watering the garden. JULIE O'NEIL: PHOTO/NATS.

Full-page photo: Harvested 'Cherry Belle' radishes. SHEPHERD OGDEN/THE COOK'S GARDEN. **Inset: A landscaped "display garden"; as pole beans grow up the supports, they shade summer greens.** SHEPHERD OGDEN/THE COOK'S GARDEN.

Full-page photo: Onions growing in rich soil.
JERRY HOWARD/POSITIVE IMAGES. **Inset: Parsley
mulched with black plastic.** JERRY HOWARD/
POSITIVE IMAGES.

Full-page photo: Companion planting with leeks and brussels sprouts. SHEPHERD OGDEN/THE COOK'S GARDEN. Inset: Tomatoes ripening on the vine. JERRY HOWARD/POSITIVE IMAGES.

Full-page photo: Swiss chard. MAGGIE OSTER. Inset: Winter rye grown as a cover crop and "green manure." JERRY HOWARD/POSITIVE IMAGES.

grow well there, and try several varieties each year until you find your favorite. Save seeds; cross-pollination is not a problem with beans.

French Horticultural (68 days to harvest; good producer) and Red Kidney (95 days; large beans) are good to eat in all three stages of growth. Try them first as snap beans, then green shelled beans, then dry beans. The large Red Kidneys are particularly versatile. Whether baked, boiled, or in soups, they're delicious. In the South, favorites are southern or Crowder peas (they are beans). They can be grown wherever lima beans do well.

BEETS

Raised throughout the United States, beets are cold-hardy, easy to grow, and resistant to insects and diseases. They prefer sunny, sandy loam, with compost well dug in. The small roots and early greens are a delicious treat, and the fall crop is easy to store. Half an ounce of seed will yield about 50 pounds of beets; a package of seed will stretch along only 2 to 3 feet of a wide-row planting. A good crop for wide rows and raised beds.

PLANTING: A beet "seed" is a really a beet "fruit," consisting of three or four seeds, so seedlings often are in clumps. Sow sparsely, 2 to 4 inches apart in narrow rows, four weeks before the last spring frost (see the map on page 77), or as early as the soil can be worked. Space narrow rows 12 to 18 inches apart. Cover seeds with ½ inch of soil. If seedlings are too thick, drag the teeth of an iron rake across the row; it will thin effectively, and the ragged-looking bed will quickly revive. When plants are 6 inches tall, thin again, to keep individual beets 4 inches apart. You can use these thinnings as tasty greens, either cooked or in a salad. Mulch seedlings in a single row. Start successive plantings two to three weeks apart for a continuous supply. For a fall crop or for storage, plant six to eight weeks before the first fall frost.

HARVESTING: Harvesting begins with thinnings when the roots are less than 1 inch in diameter and the beets are at their sweet, tender best. Beets become woody if left in the ground after maturity. If you're growing in a wide row, keep picking the earliest beets, giving the remainder space to grow. When harvesting beets for storage, leave ½ inch of the stem attached to avoid bleeding. For winter storage, plant late, leave the beets in the ground until after the first light frost, then harvest them

and store them in a cold place (35°-40° F.) with high humidity.
Try storing them in plastic bags that have ventilation holes.
Beets are easily canned or frozen, and a real treat when pickled.
In the South, gardeners can cover a row of late beets with a foot
of mulch, then dig up the beets as needed. This works in the
North, too, when the winter is mild.

VARIETIES: For an early crop, try Early Wonder (55 days to
harvest; flattened, globe-shaped) and Crosby's Egyptian (56
days; dark red, tasty). For a later crop or for fall planting for
storage, plant Detroit Dark Red (60 days; dark red and sweet).
Lutz Green Leaf (80 days) is a big beet that can be eaten either
large or small, and is a good keeper; it also has luscious greens
that taste a lot like chard.

SUGGESTION: Try growing a variety of golden beets. Many people
prefer their sweet, mild flavor and smooth, tender texture.
Some children who "hate beets" will eat these beets and love
them.

BROCCOLI

For a tasty vegetable that's loaded with nutrition, be sure to
grow broccoli. It's a fine source of vitamins A, B, and C, and can
be grown throughout the United States. It requires a loose, rich
soil that will hold moisture. Broccoli likes to mature in cool
weather, so aim for an early summer and a fall crop, and forget
about midsummer, when broccoli blossoms—or *bolts*—quickly.

PLANTING: For the best broccoli, start seeds indoors so that you
can get the plants outside in five weeks. Many people let the
plants get much bigger, but this only results in slow production
and button-sized heads. Broccoli is hardy and can be moved
outside before the last frost of the spring. In a wide row, place
the plants 16 inches apart in a 2-1-2 pattern. For a fall crop, start
plants 10 to 12 weeks before the first fall frost.

CULTIVATION: Broccoli is shallow-rooted, so cultivate carefully to
avoid damaging the roots. Mulch to preserve moisture, since
plants need a continuous supply. Side-dress with a high-
nitrogen fertilizer about 15 days after plants are set out, then
again when heads begin to form.

HARVESTING: Broccoli is grown for its flower-bud clusters, and the
tender stems near them. Cut clusters with a 4- to 6-inch stalk
before the buds open. After that head is cut, small clusters will

form in the leaf axils, and these, too, may be harvested. Broccoli freezes well.

ENEMIES: If the danger of eating cabbage worms has kept you from growing broccoli, try it again, and spray or dust with *Bacillus thuringiensis*, which is sold under the brand names Dipel, Thuricide, and Biotrol. It's a naturally occurring bacterium that's harmless to all but the worms. Start spraying when the first white butterflies flutter into the garden, and keep spraying every seven to ten days until the end of the harvest.

VARIETIES: Premium Crop (60 days from time of transplant to harvest; deep blue-green; disease-resistant; good fresh or frozen) and Green Comet (50 days; deep blue-green; holds its shape well).

BRUSSELS SPROUTS

While other vegetables are killed by the first fall frosts, brussels sprouts are only improved. Aim for a late fall crop, and pick them long after the first snowfall. Because of their hardiness, brussels sprouts are almost a perennial in the South, where the sprouts can be collected throughout the winter. Many people who dislike this vegetable have only tasted summer sprouts or overcooked sprouts, both of which taste like very strong cabbage.

PLANTING: Plan on a mid-fall harvest, allowing 30 to 45 days from seed to transplant, and 75 days from transplant to harvest. In the North, many gardeners sow seeds in a small area of the garden around June 1. A month later, they can be transplanted into wide rows, with the first sprouts ready for harvest in mid-September. Count on 25 plants in a 50-foot row to yield more than 25 pounds of sprouts. Or set the plants in a staggered formation in a wide row, placing the plants 16 to 18 inches apart.

> ### GROWING TIP
>
> To avoid disease problems, don't plant broccoli or any other cabbage family member in the same place more than once every four years. Keep cutting the side shoots, and the plants will keep producing. The fall broccoli crop often requires less spraying.

CULTIVATION: Brussels sprouts need lots of moisture, so mulch them heavily. Because their roots are near the surface of the ground, don't hoe deeply.

HARVESTING: If you miscalculate and raise summer sprouts, harvest them when they're tiny and you can still enjoy them. In the fall, as your correctly timed plants have their first sprouts, break off the lower leaves, to allow more room for sprouts. As you harvest from the bottom of the plant up, continue to take off leaves, which will stimulate the plant to grow taller and produce more sprouts. Brussels sprouts taste best after they've been nipped by frost.

Cooking Tip

One of the finest ways to enjoy brussels sprouts is to pick a batch of the smallest ones, early in the season, and add them to tossed salads or coleslaw. When cooking sprouts, cut an X with a knife in the bottom of each sprout. This ensures even cooking.

ENEMIES: See under Enemies, in the Broccoli entry, for the sure way to rid your cole crops of cabbage worms. To avoid disease problems, don't plant brussels sprouts, or any other members of the cabbage family, in the same area of the garden more than once every four years.

VARIETIES: Jade Cross (80 days from time of transplant to harvest; uniform, firm sprouts; disease-resistant) and Long Island Improved (90 days; tight heads).

Cabbage

Giant cabbages win blue ribbons at the county fair, but smaller ones make more sense in the kitchen, where a 5-pound head is about right for a single meal. Plant cabbages closer together than the seed packets and other books advise. You'll get smaller heads, but more of them in the same amount of space.

PLANTING: Start transplants inside the house four to six weeks before the date of the expected last frost (see the map on page 77). Harden off, then plant outside as much as two weeks before the frost date. In a 20-inch wide row, set in 3-2-3 formation; in a 16-inch row, set in 2-1-2 formation, with plants 10 to 12 inches apart. In narrow rows, set plants 10 to 12 inches apart. Plant in rich, moist soil, with compost added. If cutworms are a common problem, wrap each stem with a 2-inch square of newspaper.

CULTIVATION: Cabbages are very shallow rooted, so hand-pull weeds under plants, and hoe only the top ½ inch of soil around the plants. Planted in wide rows, there's little problem with weeds. If cabbages show signs of cracking, twist the heads to break some of the roots and thus slow the growing process.

HARVESTING: For a long season of eating enjoyment, begin harvesting when cabbages reach softball size. In fall, cabbages are improved by light frost, but should be stored before heavy frosts come. Cabbages can be stored in a cool cellar for as long as two months. Bring them in as late as possible, and wrap them in newspapers.

ENEMIES: The white butterfly, so innocent-looking in its flight around cabbage plants, is the worst enemy, since it signals the impending arrival of the cabbage worm. The use of *Bacillus thuringiensis* is described under Broccoli Enemies. Red varieties of cabbages have fewer cabbage worm problems.

If cabbages grow too fast, the top of the heads may be split open. At first sign of this, give the head a twist, half way around. **This breaks off some roots, and slows growth.**

VARIETIES: Early varieties include Stonehead (67 days from transplant to maturity; 4-pound heads); Emerald Cross (64 days; 4- to 5-pound heads); Golden Acre (64 days; 4- to 5-pound heads); and Early Round Dutch (71 days; firm and round, slow to split, with 4- to 5-pound heads). A midseason variety is Burpee's Copenhagen Market (72 days; 4- to 5-pound heads). Late varieties include Danish Ballhead (105 days; round, very firm heads) and Eastern Ballhead (95 days; 6- to 7-pound heads). Red cabbages well worth trying are Ruby Ball (68 days; extra early, firm, round, dark red heads) and Resistant Red Acre (76 days; deep red, good for early yield). A popular Savoy cabbage is Savoy King (90 days; good fall producer with 4- to 5-pound heads).

CARROTS

America's favorite root crop, and a great wide-row crop. In the South, carrots are grown in the fall, winter, and spring. In the North, they're a summer crop. Because carrots are used in so many ways — in salads, soups, stews, and other dishes — it's difficult to raise too many. Small carrots, rarely found in the supermarket, are most useful in the kitchen, and freeze well. Carrots grow best in rich, mellow, deeply worked soil, and so are ideal for raised beds. Fresh manure makes carrots grow hairy roots, so don't use it on them.

PLANTING: Use an empty garlic powder bottle to sow carrot seeds. This is an easy way to scatter them evenly over a wide row. Cover with ¼ inch of fine soil. If sown too thickly, pull a steel rake across the row just once, about ½ to ¾ inch into the soil. This thins the planting and removes many of the weeds that are just emerging.

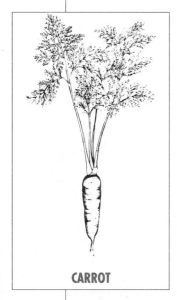

CARROT

CULTIVATION: Sow a few icicle radishes in the row with your carrots. They come up quickly, provide an early harvest, and cultivate within the row when they're removed. Carrots planted in a wide row quickly blanket the row, and discourage most weeds.

HARVESTING: The second thinning begins the true harvest, since you wait until the carrots are finger-thick, then thin them to eat. This thinning gives the remaining plants space to grow, since those that are left are 2 inches apart.

ENEMIES: Carrots are usually free of enemies. If tiny holes are found in the root, it is the work of the larvae of the carrot rust fly. Avoid planting where celery or carrots were grown previously, and sprinkle wood ashes in the row. If the problem is a continuing one, avoid planting an early crop for one year. A crop planted after June 1 will avoid the larval cycle of this fly.

VARIETIES: Long, slim varieties should be grown in deep, loose, sandy soil, chunky ones are great in heavier soils. Good choices are Chantenay Long (60 days to maturity; long and tapered); Short n' Sweet (68 days; will grow in heavy soil); and Danvers 125 (65 days; one of the tastiest varieties).

CAULIFLOWER

If you've had trouble raising cauliflower, try raising it as a fall crop. This fussiest member of the cabbage family requires a deep, rich loam, an abundance of organic material in the soil, cool temperatures, lots of moisture, ample fertilizer, and a little luck to raise a good crop. Set 25 plants in a 50-foot single row, or plant in a 3-2-3 formation in a 20-inch wide row, with plants 10 to 12 inches apart.

PLANTING: To grow as a fall crop, you want to harvest these plants as close as you can to the expected first fall frost date (see the map on page 78). Plant seeds in a small part of the garden in mid-

---

FOUR WAYS TO STORE CARROTS

- *In the garden,* heavily mulching the top and sides of the row with at least a foot of hay or leaves. Mulch heavily or the carrots will lose their crunch. Eat them soon after digging them up or they'll spoil.

- *In the refrigerator,* if you have room. They'll keep for several months in plastic bags.

- *In a box, in a cool room.* Dig the carrots, let them dry for an hour in the sun, then snip off the tops. Place a 4-inch layer of dampened sand or peat moss in the bottom of a big box. Put in a single layer of carrots, keeping them 2 inches from the sides of the box. Cover with a ½-inch layer of dampened peat moss, then fill the box, alternating layers of peat moss and carrots. Top with 6 inches of peat moss.

- *In plastic garbage bags,* in which you've punched holes. Store in a cool root cellar, or a basement, closet, or garage.

June and transplant to a wide row about five or six weeks later. When transplanting, try to disturb the roots as little as possible, and keep the young plants well supplied with water.

CULTIVATION: Cultivate lightly to avoid disrupting shallow roots. A heavy mulch around the plants conserves moisture and tends to keep the soil cooler; the plants respond with good growth. When the cauliflower heads are about 2 inches in diameter, it's time to blanch them to keep them sweet and white. Do this by bending leaves over the head, and tucking them in on the other side until the head is well hidden. Cauliflower is ready to eat four to ten days after this point. Keep it well watered during this final stage.

HARVESTING: If you've managed to bring cauliflower plants to a fruitful maturity, don't spoil it all by delaying the harvest. At this time the heads may be 6 to 12 inches across. If the individual buds of the head begin to loosen, the head is called "ricey," and it has passed its prime.

ENEMIES: Cabbage worms will dine on cauliflower. Spoil their dinner with the method described under Broccoli Enemies. If cutworms are a problem, wrap the stem of each transplant with a 2-inch square of newspaper as a cutworm collar.

VARIETIES: Early Snowball (60 days from transplant to maturity) and Burpeeana (58 days; a dependable snowball variety).

Celery

Celery isn't hard to grow. The trick is to grow celery that isn't so strong-tasting that it is only fit for flavoring soups, stews, and sauces. Widely dependable, celery is grown as a winter crop in the Deep South, an early spring or late fall crop in slightly cooler climes, and as a late summer crop in the North. Rich, moist soil should be prepared with a quantity of rotted manure or compost worked into the growing area. Figure on 100 plants per 50-foot single row, or a few more planted in two trenches in a 25-foot wide row or on top of a raised bed.

CELERY

PLANTING: Soak seeds overnight to speed germination. Start the seeds indoors 10 to 12 weeks before the last spring frost (see the map on page 77), either giving them lots of room in a flat or transplanting them once while still indoors. About two weeks after the last frost, dig a trench 6 inches deep, and plant the transplants in the bottom of the trench, 10 inches apart and set ½ inch deeper than the level at which they were growing before. As the plants grow, fill in the trench with sandy soil. Celery can be grown in two trenches stretched along a wide row or raised bed.

CULTIVATION: To keep celery from getting stringy and strong-tasting, keep it evenly moist, well fed, and blanched. A side-dressing of fertilizer will help, as will extra water in the trench whenever a dry spell threatens. The plants have short, shallow roots, so both moisture and food must be made readily available to the plants. There are many blanching methods, such as using boards and milk cartons. Probably the easiest way is to bank the plants with a sandy soil. The soil can be pulled up as high as the foliage. Washing off the soil after harvesting is not a problem; just separate the stalks and wash them with a brush under running water.

HARVESTING: It is possible, as the celery grows, to dig down and pick some of the outer stalks. The plant will continue to grow and expand. Later in the season, it is easier to harvest the entire plant.

VARIETIES: Giant Pascal (135 days from the date plants are placed in the garden); Fordhook (130 days; good as a fall crop and for winter storage); and Tendercrisp (100 days; good for short-season areas).

CORN

Corn is one of the best reasons for having a home garden. It needs a lot of space and, being a hungry crop, requires a fertile, warm, and well-drained but moist soil. Good gardeners ensure a supply that lasts for weeks by planting varieties that mature on different dates, with the latest varieties usually being the tastiest.

PLANTING: Plant each variety in short blocks for better pollination —at least four rows wide, rather than in single long rows. Make furrows with a hoe, 1 to 2 inches deep and 30 inches apart. If space is a problem, plant double rows 10 inches apart, with 30 inches between the double rows. If drainage is a problem, plant double rows on raised beds. Sow seeds 4 to 5 inches apart. Pat in place with the back of the hoe, pull soil over the seeds, then firm with the back of the hoe. Once up, thin plants to 8 to 10 inches apart.

CULTIVATION: Keep young plants free of weeds by hoeing carefully: corn roots are very shallow. Hill every two weeks, pulling soil up around the plants. This anchors the corn in a windstorm and buries the weeds. Side-dress with fertilizer when the corn is knee-high and again when it tassels. With a hoe, make a shallow furrow 6 inches from the plants, sprinkle in a thin line of fertilizer, about 1 tablespoon of 10-10-10 per plant, and cover with soil.

HARVESTING: The common advice is to have the water boiling before you pick the corn. Equally important is to pick corn when it has reached its proper maturity. Ears too immature to eat have small kernels with watery juice. Next comes the "milk stage," when the kernels become plump and sweet and make the best eating. The ear finally reaches the "dough stage," when the sugars turn to starch and the corn is unfit to eat. Pick corn when the silks first become brown and the ends of the ears feel blunt, not pointed.

ENEMIES: Plant seeds treated with fungicide to avoid damping-off, especially in cool, moist soil. If birds are a problem, buy 1-inch mesh chicken wire, 12 inches wide. Partially fold it in center, then place this tent over the row. Raccoons are masters at detecting exactly when corn is ready. Before they attack, spread moth crystals at the ends of rows and along the outer rows. Coons dislike the taste of them. Or try one of the many ways to discourage coons (for a few suggestions refer to page 43). An electric fence, carefully placed, is one of the best methods.

GROWING TIP

If wind knocking down your corn is a problem, try digging a 6-inch trench with a hoe, planting in it, then filling in the trench as corn grows. Later, hill, as described above. Or, far easier, plant the stockier varieties.

VARIETIES: Experiment to match your growing conditions and your tastes to the best varieties. Some favorites include Sugar and Gold (67 days; tender, sweet kernels; great for short seasons); Butter and Sugar (73 days; a favorite hybrid with delicious white and yellow kernels); Silver Queen (92 days; tops for eating); and Golden Bantam (80 days; an old favorite, and deservedly so).

CUCUMBERS

This warm-weather annual vine crop is grown throughout the United States. Cukes prefer fertile loam improved with well-rotted manure or compost. One-quarter ounce of seed in a 50-foot row will yield 50 pounds of cucumbers.

PLANTING: At least a week after the last frost, in a 6-inch-deep furrow, spread a couple inches of compost or a bit of commercial fertilizer and cover with soil reaching to within an inch of the top of the furrow. Spread seeds every 8 inches, firm into the soil with the back of a hoe, then cover with soil and firm again. The furrow must be in an area where the cucumber vines will have 6 feet of running space.

CULTIVATION: Side-dress with fertilizer when the vines reach stand-up stage. Keep the soil moist at all times.

HARVESTING: Cucumbers begin producing six to seven weeks after planting. Vines will produce until frost if cucumbers are picked before they reach yellow-ripe maturity — so keep them picked, even if they are not needed immediately. Early staminate or male blossoms appear first, and these do not produce cucumbers. Small cucumbers can be seen below pistillates, or female blossoms. Pick slicing cucumbers when 6 to 8 inches long, or even earlier, when there's something to eat.

ENEMIES: Cucumber beetles, both striped and 12-spotted, will eat young plants and dine on the leaves and stems of larger plants. Use malathion to control them. Hot caps or cheesecloth on frames over each plant will protect young plants. Fungal diseases like downy mildew can be avoided by rotation of crops, control of insects, and selection of resistant seeds.

VARIETIES: Varieties include both slicing and pickling cucumbers such as Marketmore 70 (65 days; produces crisp, flavorful, 8-inch slicing cucumbers); Straight 8 (58 days; slicing; does well in the North); Spartan Valour (60 days; slicing; very slim, dark, and prolific); and Wisconsin SMR 18 (54 days; pickling; good yielder; scab- and mosaic-resistant).

EGGPLANT

Eggplant is fussy, but it's a delight for any gourmet and is worth growing, if only for the beauty of its fruit. Eggplant is very sensitive to cold weather, but this should not deter the home gardener — it makes a good experimental crop for the gardener who has never tried it. Eggplant needs rich soil, with compost or rotted manure added. One packet of seeds should produce 50 plants, double the number needed for even a family of eggplant lovers.

PLANTING: Start seeds indoors ¼ inch deep in flats or in 3-inch peat pots, seven to eight weeks in advance of transplanting time (about a week after the last spring frost, when the soil is warm). Set plants out in the garden 12 inches apart in rows 2 to 3 feet apart. Plant in a 2-1-2 formation in a wide row. Shade the plants for a day or two after planting.

CULTIVATION: Eggplants must be kept warm, moist, and fed from the moment you plant the seeds. Their growth pattern should not be interrupted by a lack of moisture or by cold. Keep weeds out of the row, side-dress the plants with compost, and mulch well, after the plants have gotten a good start in warm soil. Don't cultivate deeply, as the roots are near the surface.

HARVESTING: Admiration of the beauty of the fruit should not delay the harvest. Begin when the fruits are small, cutting them from the stem. If the fruits are left until they lose their gloss, the taste will suffer and the plant will stop producing.

ENEMIES: The Colorado potato beetle will desert potato vines to feast on your eggplants. Try dusting with rotenone as a deterrent. Discourage cutworms by placing paper collars around the stems. To avoid bacterial wilt, don't grow eggplants in a spot where potatoes, tomatoes, or eggplants have grown in the past three years.

VARIETIES: Black Beauty is the favorite (73 days from transplant to first mature fruit; good producer of heavy, oval fruit). Ichiban (65 days) is a prolific producer of long and early fruit. To understand how eggplant got its name, grow a few of the ones that bear small, white fruit. Try Albino, Ornamental White, or White Beauty; they're fine to eat as well as being decorative.

LEEKS

Leeks require a long season to reach the size of those found in markets. Don't despair if yours are smaller — they're just as tasty, and often are more tender. Leeks look like oversize green onions. They must be blanched to achieve that white lower stem so favored by the best cooks.

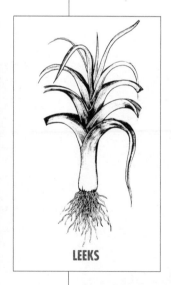

LEEKS

PLANTING: To give leeks a good start in the North, sow seeds in flats, 1 inch apart and ½ inch deep, three months before the last frost. Keep the tops cut back. Tranplant them about the time of the last frost, at the bottom of a 6-inch-deep furrow. Space them 4 to 6 inches apart, and plant them 1 inch deeper than the level at which they were growing before. You can make two of these furrows running length-wise on a raised bed or wide row. In the South, you can sow seeds or set out transplants in the fall.

CULTIVATION: Gradually fill in the furrow as the leeks grow, to blanch them and make them more tender. As they reach full growth, bank the entire stem with sand or compost. If plants are in a wide row or raised bed, it's possible to add several inches of compost, soil, or leaves to blanket the bed.

HARVESTING: If you have a lot of leeks, harvest some of them early in the summer as scallions, or use them as leeks, adding five small ones for every big one called for in a recipe. For late fall use, leeks may be left in the ground until after a heavy frost, then dug, packed closely, and stored in an unheated building or garage. Late-started crops can be overwintered by mulching heavily with hay or straw; they produce a delicious spring crop.

ENEMIES: Leeks have few enemies, and are easily grown. If rot is detected, onion maggot (the larva of a small, gray fly) may be responsible. Destroy any plants showing symptoms of rot.

VARIETIES: American Flag (120 days to maturity; fine for fall and winter) and Broad London (130 days; good in the South).

Lettuce

Loose-Leaf Lettuce

Raise just a little lettuce — but at a lot of different times. If you plant different varieties and start lettuce at two-week intervals, you'll have top-quality lettuce for the table at all times. Lettuce does best in cool temperatures — spring and fall — in rich, well-watered soil.

PLANTING: To eat homegrown lettuce as early in the season as possible, start seeds indoors six weeks before the last spring frost. When the ground can be worked, transplant outside, and at the same time plant seeds outdoors. Lettuce is an ideal crop for raised beds and wide rows. Set out transplants in a 3-2-3 formation, 8 inches apart. Cover seeds with ¼ inch of soil.

GROWING TIP

In hot weather, grow plants in the shade — on the north side of a cucumber trellis, behind towering bean poles, or under bean tepees or broccoli plants. Or stretch cheesecloth across a section of a wide-row planting.

Raise only short sections of a wide row or raised bed, such as 3 to 5 feet for each variety, or about 20 feet for any variety in a single row. In late summer start the fall crop.

CULTIVATION: Thin the seeded section of the wide row to give remaining plants room to grow. Keep the soil moist and the ground free of weeds, so that growth isn't interrupted.

HARVESTING: Begin harvesting as soon as the leaves are big enough to eat. To get the maximum amount of lettuce, cut off the leaves an inch above the ground. That way, you'll get at least two harvests from the same plant, as plants send up new growth. If it's cool and damp, you may get as many as five harvests. Lettuce is crispest in the morning, the best time to harvest.

ENEMIES: Rot at the base of plants is usually due to overcrowding. Rotate plantings to avoid fungal and bacterial diseases. Slugs dislike scatterings of wood ashes or lime, and will drown in saucers of beer placed around the bed.

VARIETIES: Try a lot of them. Some of the best are Salad Bowl (45 days to maturity; crisp and tender; almost foolproof); Black-Seeded Simpson (45 days; great taste); Ruby (50 days; adds color to your garden and your salad bowl); and Oak Leaf (40 days; one of the more heat-resistant of leaf lettuces).

HEAD LETTUCE

There are two main varieties of head lettuce — the crisphead types, so common in the supermarket, and butterheads, with looser, greener heads and more taste and vitamins. You can grow both in your garden, although crispheads may be less perfect than the commercial varieties. Crispheads are more difficult to grow, but you can get a good crop if you start early and harvest before hot weather arrives.

Try planting head lettuce in this formation.

PLANTING: Start head lettuce seeds inside, six weeks before the last expected frost, which is the ideal time to set out transplants. Set them in a 3-2-3 formation in a wide row, 8 to 10 inches apart. In midsummer, start a fall crop of butterhead lettuce. In the South, gardeners aiming for a fall crop sow seed in early August and transplant as soon as the plants are large enough. The bed should be partially shaded and kept well watered; the crop will head from late October to late December. For a spring crop in the South, sow lettuce in cold frames from early November to late January, depending on the location and weather. Plants are set out from January to March and harvest begins two months later.

CULTIVATION: Mulch with compost to keep weeds down. Keep the lettuce well watered. Wide rows keep the soil cool, and cool soil is what lettuce loves.

HARVESTING: Harvest some heads before they reach full growth, to give others in the wide row room to expand.

ENEMIES: See under Loose-Leaf Lettuce.

VARIETIES: A small sample of the many excellent varieties available includes Ithaca (90 days); Great Lakes (90 days; heavy crisphead type; good quality; stands up well to heat); Buttercrunch (75 days; a superior butterhead; tasty, crisp, and slow to bolt); and Dark Green Boston (80 days).

MUSKMELON

The perfect melon, juicy and tasty, is the dream of many gardeners, and it's just as elusive, too. That perfect melon must be the right variety for your area, and it demands a good start in the spring: a rich, moist, sandy soil; room enough to stretch out vines; freedom from disease and insects; and a long season of sunny, warm weather and tropical nights. If you have clay soil, try preparing raised beds, adding lots of compost and organic matter to the soil. A 50-foot row should yield about 30 melons.

MUSKMELON

PLANTING: Start seeds indoors in peat pots, three weeks before planting time. This lengthens the short seasons of the North, and lets melons ripen before the hot, dry periods in the South. Plant outside a week after the last frost date, when the soil is warm. Carefully remove the peat pots before planting, being careful not to disturb the roots. Plant in rows 10 to 12 inches apart; space the rows 6 feet apart. Protect, if necessary, with hot caps or plastic grow tunnels.

CULTIVATION: Melons are shallow-rooted, so cultivate carefully and mulch when the soil is warm. Avoid moving vines. Remove melon fruits that set late in the season, to improve the size and quality of the earlier ones. To hasten growing and ripening, set small melons on coffee cans or mulch with black plastic, which tends to keep the soil warmer and produce earlier melons.

HARVESTING: Muskmelons are ready to be eaten when they are at "slip" stage (when slight pressure on the vine causes the melon to slip off). Some gardeners kneel down and sniff the end of the fruit for the rich, fruity smell that tells them the melon is ready to pick.

ENEMIES: Starting melons indoors lessens the chance of trouble from striped cucumber beetle, which attacks seedlings and spreads fusarium wilt. Hot caps, fine for warming the area around plants, will also help protect them from these beetles. Downy and powdery mildew are worse in wet weather. Varieties tolerant to both mildew and wilt are available.

VARIETIES: Remember to find out which melons do best in your area. Honeydews, for example, love the hot, dry climate of the Southwest, but don't produce as well in the South. Favorite varieties are Ambrosia (86 days; very sweet, with thick meat) and Alaska (70 days; an early producer that's tops in flavor).

NOTE: In this country, almost any muskmelon is called a cantaloupe, but the truth is they're not the same. True cantaloupes have hard, warted rinds and are seldom grown in the United States. With their netted, yellow or green skins, muskmelons have assumed the identity of their European cousin.

Onions

Onions are essential in any garden. They grow anywhere in the United States, and produce well in limited space. Rare is the gardener who raises too many. When planning for storage, remember that the stronger its flavor, the longer an onion will keep. Fertile, moist soil is needed to grow onions. The gardener has a choice of raising onions from seeds, plants, or sets (tiny onions started the previous season).

PLANTING: Seeds should be started indoors 10 to 12 weeks in advance of transplanting. Start seeds in a flat with 4 to 5 inches of soil or starter mix.

CULTIVATION: Keep the onions free of weeds, particularly when first started. Side-dress with fertilizer when the shoots are 6 to 8 inches high, and again when bulbs begin to form.

HARVESTING: Pull up onions when their tops turn brown and leave them in the garden for two or three sunny days, until they are dry. Then break off the roots. To cure the onions, spread them out in a warm, airy, shaded place until the roots are dry and brittle and the skin becomes papery. Eat thick-stemmed onions first — they won't keep as long. Put others in a mesh bag and hang in a cool, dry area. When cutting off the tops, leave about an inch at the neck.

ENEMIES: It is not often that the home gardener is troubled with either pests or diseases in the onion row. Onion maggot, a tiny, white, wormlike creature, may attack seedlings, making them rot. If they invade larger onions that are stored, they can cause a rot that will spread to others. Destroy onions where this is detected.

VARIETIES: In the North, try Early Yellow Globe (100 days; good for either a summer or fall crop) or Southport Yellow Globe (115 days). In the South try Granex (105 days; early yellow bulb; a good keeper) or Texas Early Grano 502 (a thrip-resistant variety). If you plant sets, try Stuttgarter (120 days) or Yellow Ebenezer (100 days).

GROWING TIP

Onions are a good companion crop. Plant a few in with other vegetables, such as lettuce, and pick them in all stages, from scallions (before they develop bulbs) to the mature onion. If you like scallions, plant onion sets only 1½ inches apart in wide rows. Harvest every other one as a scallion. The rest will develop into larger onions.

PEAS

Peas can be grown in most parts of the United States, but do best in cool climates. They are one of the best crops for wide rows and raised beds, and prefer growing in rich, sandy loam. One-half pound of planted peas should yield at least 30 pounds of fresh peas. Tall varieties require support, such as a fence or branches 4 to 5 feet long.

PLANTING: Dust seed with a nitrogen-fixing inoculant (available from most seed suppliers) before planting. As soon as the ground can be worked, plant seeds 1 inch deep, spaced 2 to 3 inches apart, spacing the rows 3 feet apart. In wide rows, scatter seeds 3 to 4 inches apart, and rake a 1-inch layer of soil over them. Soaking peas before planting is recommended only if the ground is dry. Instead of successive plantings for a longer harvest, plant early and later varieties at the same time. In wide rows, plant short-stemmed varieties, such as Little Marvel and Progress #9, that require no support.

CULTIVATION: Keep weeds out of the young plants. Irrigate if spring rains don't provide enough moisture, and make certain there is enough moisture in the critical period when the pods are filling out. Mulch the rows.

HARVESTING: Harvest when the pods are young and tender— as soon as they are well filled, but before they begin to turn color. Shell and cook the peas as soon after picking as possible.

ENEMIES: Malathion will halt any aphids that cause trouble, which is rare.

VARIETIES: Experiment each year until you find the ideal pea for your soil conditions, climate, and taste, recording your successes and failures. Some good bets include Little Marvel (63 days from planting to eating; 18-inch high bushes; tasty both fresh and frozen); Progress #9 (60 days; resistant to fusarium wilt; productive and delicious); and Lincoln (75 days; for the gourmet who will wait a few days for the best).

SUGGESTION: For a hedge of peas, try Novella in a row that's as wide as your rake. This leafless variety forms a neat hedge that looks as if it has been clipped. The Novella peas are delicious.

PEPPERS

Grow lots of these, and try different varieties. There are the hot ones that seem grow hotter as they change color, and the blocky fruit varieties, called sweet, bell, or green peppers. The sweet pepper is usually eaten green, but its vitamin-C content increases if it's left on the plant to turn red. Peppers prefer a mellow loam, but do well in any fertile, well-drained soil. One plant will often yield a pound or more of peppers. Try planting a wide row of peppers, aligned in a 3-2-3 formation, 12 to 14 inches apart, or a narrower wide row in a 2-1-2 formation.

PLANTING: Start plants indoors six to eight weeks in advance of transplanting time, which is at least one week after the last spring frost (see the map on page 77). Start in flats or in 3-inch peat pots, planting seeds ½ inch deep. Set out plants 12 to 14 inches apart, in rows 30 inches apart, or in wide rows or raised beds. Water well and, if sunny and hot, shade after transplanting. Relatively quick-growing crops, such as radishes or green onions, can be planted with peppers and harvested before the pepper plants reach their full growth.

CULTIVATION: Peppers develop at their own pace, and the gardener should not worry if at times the plants seem to do nothing for days. After the ground is warm, mulch to keep down weeds and conserve moisture. Some gardeners recommend using black plastic mulch — it tends to make soil warmer, and warm soil is what peppers like. Plants may need watering in the first few weeks after being set out, but usually not after that time.

HARVESTING: Both sweet and hot peppers are good to eat at all stages of growth. Cut peppers off the plants with a knife or scissors, ½ inch above the pepper cap. Sweet varieties are excellent for freezing.

ENEMIES: Use newspaper collars around tiny plants to thwart cutworms. Most other troubles can be prevented if you keep the plants weeded and don't walk around the plants when they're wet. If you have husky, dark green pepper plants and no peppers, you've probably overfed them with a nitrogen-rich fertilizer. If they have blossoms, but don't bear peppers, blame that on a cold spell and wait for further blossoms. All peppers should be side-dressed when they blossom. For instructions, see the side-dressing information on page 38. Limit the amount of commercial fertilizer used to a teaspoon per plant.

VARIETIES: A wide range of peppers is available, including Gedeon (78 days; huge, elongated fruit; a sweet variety that's great for stuffing or freezing); California Wonder (75 days; sweet); Sweet Banana (72 days; yellow to orange-red); Sweet

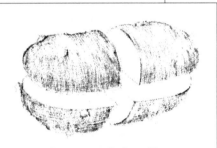

Cut seed potatoes into chunks, each having two or three buds.

Cherry (78 days; great for pickling whole); Long Red Cayenne (72 days; hot; easily dried); and Hungarian Wax (65 days; hot yellow, changing to red, with 6-inch fruit).

POTATOES

Garden books often suggest that home gardeners should not raise potatoes, since they take up a lot of room and, unlike corn, peas, or tomatoes, aren't much better than store-bought varieties. But this means you'll miss the taste of small new potatoes, and the surprise in the fall of digging into each hill to see how many there will be. Try planting ten pounds and judge for yourself. Potatoes need mellow, fertile, acid, well-drained soil, that has neither been limed nor fertilized with fresh manure. Five pounds of potatoes planted in a 50-foot row should produce more than 50 pounds.

PLANTING: Two days before planting, cut seed potatoes (for best results, make sure they're certified seed potatoes) into blocky chunks, each with at least two eyes. Dig 8-inch-deep trenches, 36 inches apart. Add a 2-inch layer of compost, plus some super phosphate fertilizer, about a handful per foot, to the bottom of the trench. Cover with 2 inches of soil. Place potato chunks cut side down, 10 to 12 inches apart. Cover with 4 inches of soil.

Growing Tips

Potatoes can withstand some insect damage, but don't let all of the foliage be eaten before taking action. Look on the undersides of leaves for bright orange dots — the eggs of the Colorado potato beetle.

Green potatoes contain solanine, which can be toxic. Remove any green parts before eating. Storing potatoes in the dark will prevent greening.

CULTIVATION: Start hilling as soon as plants emerge. Pull soil into the trench around the growing plants, then cover them right up. Hilling kills the weeds, allows developing tubers to expand, and keeps emerging potatoes from turning green in the sun. Do this at least twice.

HARVESTING: Two weeks after blossoms form, start harvesting some of those small, early potatoes — they're delicious. For storage, allow the potatoes to mature and harvest when most of the tops have died back. Dig them up when the soil is dry. Dry potatoes for a few hours outside, then store them in a dark room with high humidity and temperatures between 36° to 40°F.

ENEMIES: Potatoes are susceptible to as many as 60 diseases. But no crop yet has had all of them, and most can be avoided by following a few rules. Don't grow potatoes where tomatoes, eggplant, or peppers (or potatoes, of course) have grown in the past three years. Don't add lime or fresh manure to the soil. Plant certified disease-free potatoes. To combat Colorado potato beetles, pick them off, or use rotenone according to instructions on the label.

VARIETIES: Plant area favorites. Some include Norland (80 days; early, red-skinned, resistant to scab); Kennebec (110 days; late maturing; an old reliable); and Katahdin (110 days; late maturing; a good keeper).

PUMPKINS

This sprawling squash plant is as intrusive as a borrowing neighbor, but you've got to raise it if there are young members in your family. Scratch their names on their "own" young pumpkins, and those names will appear large and plain at Halloween. As a space-saving maneuver, interplant with sweet corn, if you don't mind tripping over the vines as you gather corn. Stronger in flavor than other squash, pumpkins are less popular for cooking, but can be used in pies and bread. They prefer growing in rich, light soil.

PLANTING: Space rows 8 to 10 feet apart. Dig in plenty of compost or well-rotted manure. Two weeks after the last frost, plant seeds 1 inch deep, 8 to 10 inches apart.

CULTIVATION: Mulch heavily and keep well watered. Once vines have set several fruits, pinch back the vines to direct growth into the fruit.

> ## GROWING TIP
>
> To save space, train pumpkin vines onto a strong fence. The vine and tendrils will grow extra strong to support the weight of the pumpkins.

HARVESTING: Pumpkins may disappear from your garden if not harvested before Halloween. After a light frost, but before a hard frost, cut them from the vines with a sharp knife, leaving a 3-inch handle. Allow them to cure for two or three weeks in a warm, well-ventilated place. Store in a cool, dry cellar.

ENEMIES: Squash vine borer can sometimes prove troublesome. If the branch of a vine wilts, cut into where the wilt begins, and dig out the borer. Check for squash bugs in the heat of the day and crush any found.

VARIETIES: Favorites include Connecticut Field (110 days; coarse, sweet meat; weighs 15 to 25 pounds); Small Sugar (100 days; excellent flavor; weighs about 7 pounds); and Cinderella (95 days; 10-inch pumpkins grow on a bushlike plant that can be restrained in an area of 6 square feet).

RADISHES

A cool-weather vegetable, radishes are grown in winter in the South, spring and fall in the North. They like rich, sandy loam. One-half ounce of seed will yield 25 pounds, but you should plant in much smaller amounts, such as a 2-foot section of a wide row, or mixed in with carrots and other vegetables, to be harvested long before their bedmates. Planted this way, radishes tend to keep weeds out of the bed, making it much easier to grow crops like carrots.

PLANTING: As soon as the soil can be worked, sow seeds about 1 inch apart in rows 1 foot apart, or in wide rows. Cover with ¼ inch of soil or sifted compost. Plant early varieties first, switch to summer varieties when the weather warms up, then switch to late varieties.

CULTIVATION: Because of their quick growing season, radishes demand little attention beyond weeding and watering.

HARVESTING: Pick radishes before or as they reach maturity. Leave late varieties in the ground until after a frost, then pull them up and store them in damp sand in the cellar.

ENEMIES: To avoid maggots, plant late; don't plant where any member of the cabbage family has grown in the past three years.

VARIETIES: Some of the best types available include Cherry Belle (22 days; early, bright red, round and smooth); Sparkler (25 days; round, red, with lower portion of root white); White Icicle (28 days; summer variety; slender roots, white skin); and Celestial (60 days; late variety; 6 to 8 inches of pure white root; good for storage).

Spinach

Spinach is a cool-weather crop, to be planted as soon as the soil can be worked, then raised quickly and harvested before it goes to seed. It's grown in the winter in the South, in the early spring and late fall in the North. Spinach will grow on any fertile, nitrogen-rich soil. Lime should be added if the soil is at all acidic. One-half ounce of seed will yield 40 pounds of spinach.

PLANTING: Spinach is a good wide-row crop, since it will shade the soil, keep it cool, and thus delay the process of going to seed that makes the plant inedible. Plant fresh seeds each year, as soon as the ground can be worked. In a row the width of a garden rake, thin plants to 3 to 4 inches apart. In narrow rows set 12 inches apart, space plants 3 to 4 inches apart. Successive plantings are recommended, stopping in midsummer, but resuming in the fall.

CULTIVATION: Little needs to be done with a wide row. For narrow rows, mulch to keep the soil cooler.

HARVESTING: Harvest early, when the plants are small, then eat the leaves raw, in a spinach salad. Cut the plants low, but leave the tiny center leaves to grow, then cut again when the plant has 4 to 6 leaves. Cut more than you think you need — spinach cooks down alarmingly. Spinach also freezes well.

ENEMIES: Plant blight-resistant varieties, keep well weeded or heavily mulched, and you'll remain blissfully ignorant of the diseases listed for this vegetable. Pick off any spinach flea beetles — ¼-inch, greenish black fellows — or their larvae, both found on the undersides of leaves.

VARIETIES: Some favorites include Melody (42 days; a vigorous plant with semi-crinkled leaves); Bloomsdale Long Standing (48 days; savoyed; resists bolting); and Early Hybrid #7 (42 days; resistant to downy mildew; semi-savoyed leaves; good for freezing and canning).

> ## GROWING TIP
>
> In most northern climates you can plant spinach in early fall and, if it is protected by a good snow cover, it will overwinter and grow in the spring.

SQUASH

SUMMER SQUASH

Prizes should be awarded to gardeners who grow no more summer squash than they can eat. There's a huge variety to choose from, so restraint in planting is essential. A truly American plant, squash grows throughout the United States, and in abundance. One-quarter pound of seed will yield at least 150 squash. Bush varieties yield more in less space. All squash like a deep, rich soil. If you live in a particularly cool climate, grow squash in a raised bed.

PLANTING: Spade well-rotted manure or compost into sandy loam. Most folks won't need to plant any more than 5 feet of each variety. Allow 4 feet between rows. When all danger of frost is past and the soil is warm, plant seeds ½ inch deep and 6 inches apart.

CULTIVATION: Keep weeded and well watered. Side-dress when buds appear. (See side-dressing instructions on page 37).

HARVESTING: Pick early and often. Summer squash is best if picked before it matures, while it is still tender and tasty. To encourage continuous production, pick off any large squash and add them to the compost pile.

ENEMIES: If given a good start, plants will nearly care for themselves. Use fresh seed, add compost to the hills, and rotate crops. Rotenone will discourage squash bugs and cucumber beetles. Squash bugs hide under shingles and boards and can be uncovered and killed early in the morning. If cucumber beetles are a problem, start squash plants indoors, or protect the plants with a tent of cheesecloth. You'll know that a squash vine borer is present if the mature vine suddenly wilts. Using a sharp knife, slit the vine back to where a white grub, the borer, will be found. Get rid of him, then cover the slit stem with soil, giving it a chance to form roots.

VARIETIES: There are more good ones than can be listed, so read seed catalogs and experiment. Try Early Prolific Straightneck (50 days; bush variety; creamy yellow fruit; harvest from 4 to 6 inches until it reaches 12 to 14 inches in length). Other good choices are White Bush Patty Pan (54 days; bush variety; deliciously mild) and Zucchini (50 days; bush variety; prolific).

WINTER SQUASH

Select several varieties, and be prepared to sacrifice a lot of space unless you choose the bush varieties. Winter squash is grown throughout the United States, each area having its favorites. Plant squash in sandy loam, adding plenty of compost or well-rotted manure. One-half ounce of seed in hills will yield 75 or more pounds of squash, depending on the variety.

GROWING TIP

Also try growing New Jersey Golden Acorn. This squash is very tasty and can be eaten as a summer squash when immature, or allowed to mature for winter squash. One drawback is that it doesn't keep as well as other winter squash, so plan to eat it up in late fall and early winter.

PLANTING: If your garden is adjacent to an uncultivated area, plant squash so that the vines can rampage out of the garden, rather than across rows of carefully cultivated crops. Plant squash in rows spaced 8 to 10 feet apart. Rows of bush varieties can be set closer, 5 to 6 feet apart. After all danger of frost is past, set seeds 5 to 6 inches apart and 1 inch deep. Squash can be started indoors in peat pots a month in advance, but great care must be taken to avoid damaging the tap root when transplanting.

CULTIVATION: Keep the soil moist. When bush squash have set 6 fruit, thin out any excess to ensure the best quality.

HARVESTING: Unlike summer squash, winter types must mature fully on the vines, attaining full growth and hardened skins, in order to store well. Before the first frost, cut squash off the vines with a sharp knife. Handle them gently, let them cure in a warm, airy, sheltered location, then store all of the sound fruit in a dry cellar, at temperatures between 40° and 50°F.

ENEMIES: See listing under Summer Squash.

VARIETIES: Experiment with several, particularly the space-saving bush varieties, to find the ones you like best. Some good ones to try are Butternut (85 days; excellent flavor, good keeper, and resistant to squash borer); Blue Hubbard (120 days; a traditional variety, with impressive 15-pound fruits not uncommon; good keeper and tasty); Gold Nugget (85 days; bush type, requires little room; small, pumpkin-shaped, bright orange fruit with deep yellow flesh; good baked in the shell); and Table Queen or Acorn (80 days; good baked in the shell, with half making one serving).

Swiss Chard

Swiss chard makes an excellent garden crop, since it sends down long, powerful roots that will break up heavy subsoil. Mellow soil, not acid, should be enriched to ensure the best crop. Only a single planting is required. One-quarter ounce of seed sparsely sown will yield 50 or more pounds of chard. A good fall crop, and an excellent crop to raise in a wide row or on a raised bed.

SWISS CHARD

If you have trouble raising spinach, or tire of seeing it suddenly go to seed with the first hot spell, try Swiss chard as a substitute. It's easy to grow, can be harvested for a long season, and its taste compares well to that of spinach (some people even like it better). Another good point is that it doesn't cook down as much as spinach will.

PLANTING: As soon as the ground can be worked, plant seeds 2 or 3 inches apart in a wide row or on a raised bed (thinning to 4 to 6 inches apart), or in narrow rows 18 inches apart, with plants spaced 3 to 4 inches apart. Plant seeds 1 inch deep. In the South, plant chard in the fall and harvest all winter.

HARVESTING: When plants are 6 inches tall, thin by removing other plants (and use them in the kitchen). When the remaining plants reach maturity, harvest by cutting back to 1 inch above the ground. Plants will grow again, and you'll get three to four harvests. In late summer, cut back all the plants and side-dress the crop, for a harvest that will last until early winter.

ENEMIES: Mexican bean beetles can be picked off by hand, and their eggs on the undersides of leaves should be crushed. Goldfinches also love this crop.

VARIETIES: Two good chards are Fordhook Giant (60 days to first cutting; emerald green with white stalks, heavily crumpled leaves) and Ruby (60 days; a beautiful, bright crimson rhubarb chard, with a sweet flavor).

TOMATOES

A must crop in every garden, no matter how small. Experiment with different varieties each year. Tomatoes grow throughout the United States, even in winter in the extreme South, and in the spring, summer, and fall further north. Just ten plants can yield 100 pounds of tomatoes. Sprawling tomato plants will produce more tomatoes, but of lesser quality, and they may attract slugs. If you have soil problems, such as clay soil or wet soil, try a raised bed for your tomatoes.

PLANTING: Most people start tomato plants far too early and end up with leggy plants when it's time to transplant them. The best transplants are no more than eight weeks old, or 8 inches high.

GROWING TIP

To get early tomatoes, start an early variety (Pixie, Coldset, or Early Girl) eight to 12 weeks before the last frost. Then set them out three to four weeks before the last frost. Enclose each plant in a wire cylinder covered with clear plastic to trap heat. If frosts threaten, cover with newspaper sheets right inside the cylinder.

A common method is to start them in flats, at temperatures between 70° and 75°F. Transplant them into 3-inch peat pots when they have true leaves, setting them deep in the pots. Keep them under fluorescent lights, at a temperature around 65°F. Harden them off by setting them outside for the ten days before you transplant them, giving them a little more sunlight every day. Transplant them in the garden on a cloudy day when all danger of frost is past, setting the plants in deeply, so that additional roots can grow along the stem. If you plan to stake the tomatoes, put the stake in at this time. Plant 3 feet apart in rows spread 4 feet apart if sprawling, or 2 feet apart in rows spaced 3 feet apart if staked or in wire cages.

CULTIVATION: Mulch heavily when the soil is warm, about the time the plants blossom. Until then, cultivate to keep weeds down and provide moisture. Remove any suckers that grow between branches.

HARVESTING: Let tomatoes ripen on the vine for best eating. Keep them picked. When frost threatens, pick green tomatoes, put them on a shelf, and cover them with sheets of newspaper. Check daily to use ripened tomatoes.

ENEMIES: Place newspaper collars around young plants when setting them out, to defeat cutworms. Search out and destroy the huge green tomato worm, or control it with *Bacillus thuringiensis*. Many diseases can be avoided by planting resistant varieties, giving plants ample room, providing plenty of moisture, and by not working around the plants when they're wet.

VARIETIES: Select tomatoes for specific uses, such as Better Boy (70 days) as the main crop, Red Cherry (72 days) or Yellow Pear (70 days) for salads, and Roma VF (72 days) for paste and sauce.

TURNIPS

This cool-weather crop is raised for both its roots and its tops. Turnips are usually grown as a summer crop in the North, and planted in July and August. In the South, they're planted in February and March; then new plantings, just for the greens, are started from July through October. Turnips like a moist, rich soil, but one that's not too heavy with nitrogen. One-quarter ounce of seed will yield about 50 pounds. They make a good wide-row crop.

PLANTING: Sow seeds very sparsely, ¼ inch deep, in wide rows or in rows spaced 18 inches apart. Moisten with a spray.

CULTIVATION: In either a single row or a raised bed, thin turnips to 3 to 5 inches apart.

HARVESTING: Use turnip thinnings as greens. Early crops may be harvested when roots are 1½ inches in diameter. Harvest the fall crop after the first frost. Cut the tops off close and store in a cool, damp location.

ENEMIES: If cabbage worms show interest in your turnips, see under Broccoli Enemies for a sure-fire way of destroying them.

VARIETIES: Some popular turnip varieties include Purple-Top White Globe (55 days; crisp and tasty; harvest when 2 to 3 inches in diameter); Purple-Top Milan (45 days; good for a spring crop); Shogoin (30 days for greens, 70 days for roots); and Tokyo Cross (45 days; white; excellent for greens).

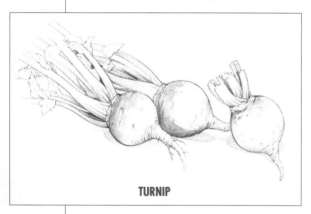

TURNIP

Mean Date of Last 32° Temperature in Spring

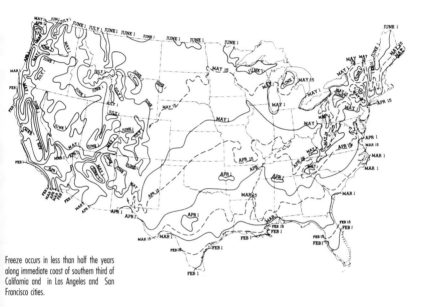

Freeze occurs in less than half the years along immediate coast of southern third of California and in Los Angeles and San Francisco cities.

Spring freezes occur south of this dotted line in less than half the years.

Spring freezes are assumed to occur between January 1 and June 30.

Caution should be used in interpolating on this generalized map. Sharp changes in the mean date may occur in short distances due to differences in altitude, slope of land, type of soil, vegetative cover, bodies of water, air, drainage, urban heat effects, etc.

MEAN DATE OF FIRST 32° TEMPERATURE
IN AUTUMN

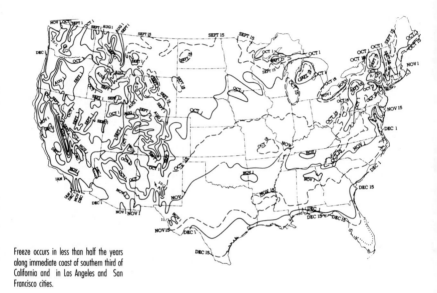

Freeze occurs in less than half the years
along immediate coast of southern third of
California and in Los Angeles and San
Francisco cities.

Fall freezes occur south of this dotted line in
less than half the years.

Autumn (fall) freezes are assumed to occur
between July 1 and December 30.

Caution should be used in interpolating on this generalized map. Sharp changes in the mean date may occur
in short distances due to differences in altitude, slope of land, type of soil, vegetative cover, bodies of water,
air, drainage, urban heat effects, etc.

Index